50 Fabric Animals

Fun sewing projects for you and your home

Search Press

Contents

Enlarging the patterns

Many of the patterns for the projects in this book have been reduced in size to fit and need to be scaled back up. Use the 5cm (2in) arrow as your guide, enlarging the patterns until the arrow measures 5cm (2in) – or the size specified beside the arrow if different. To do this, work as follows:

To avoid confusion, the example here is given in metric measurements only. First, measure the bar, e.g. 1.5cm, then carry out the following calculation: 5 divided by 1.5 = 3.33. Multiply by 100 to get the percentage you need. If the answer is less than 200%, you can go ahead and enlarge your pattern(s) to full size straight away. However, the rate of enlargement for this example is 333%.

Photocopies cannot enlarge by more than 200%, so first enlarge to 200%. For the second enlargement, carry out the following calculation:

333 divided by 200 = 1.66. Again, multiply your answer by 100 to get the percentage you need. The percentage of the second enlargement is 166%.

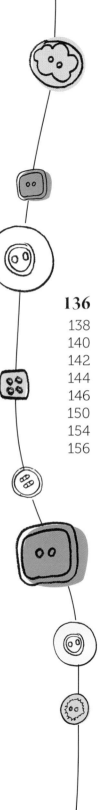

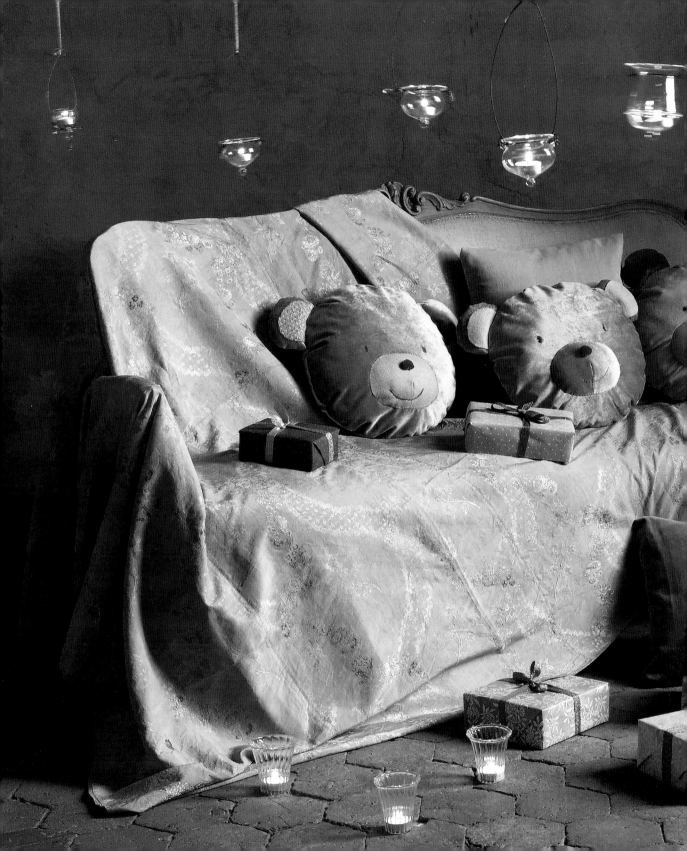

Traditional designs

Traditional designs

Big bear

Dimensions

Approximately 55cm (21¾in) tall

Materials

Remnants of woollen fabrics, tweeds and cottons plus second-hand knitted garments and socks (felted or not) in chocolate, taupe and grey shades ● synthetic (or mohair) plush fabric for the backs of the ears ● cotton lining for all knitted pieces ● pair of 2mm (½in) glass bear eyes ● set of five 40mm (1½in) metal/card bear joints ● standard-size cotter-pin key for use with the bear joints ● 1kg (2lb) stuffing ● long tapestry needle ● thick black embroidery cotton ● matching thread

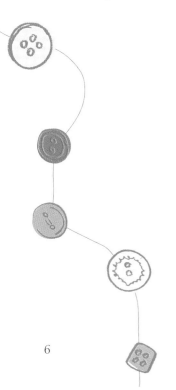

Method

Enlarge the patterns on page 9 to size (see page 2) and cut them out to obtain templates. Select the fabrics for each bear piece, joining scraps if necessary to obtain the correct size. Use plush fabric for two ear pieces (backs of the ears). Cut out the pieces, adding 1cm (⅜in) all round each one for seam allowances. Cut the legs, and other pieces that need to be cut in pairs, from folded fabic. When using unfelted knitted fabrics, cut the patterns again from cotton fabric and tack the cotton fabric to the back of the knitted one as a lining. When joining, place all pieces together with right sides facing, taking up the lining at the same time, where applicable. Mark the reference points of the patterns with pins or tacking.

Head and body Join the two side-head pieces from the base of the front neck to the tip of the nose. Stitch the centre head between the two side-head pieces, starting at the nose; turn out. Join the top front (body) to the bottom front. Close up the dart on the top front up to B. Close up the dart on the bottom-front piece too. Join the two back pieces along the centre back, leaving the opening free. Join the front and back all round, leaving only the middle of the back open and then turn out.

Arms and legs Join each inside arm to a palm. Join each inside arm to an outside arm, stitching all round but leaving an opening for the filling and to fix the joints; turn out. Join the legs together in pairs, leaving the bottom open and the gap at the back for stuffing. Stitch the sole to each leg, starting at the heel; turn out.

Ears Join each plush ear to a contrasting ear around the curved edge, leaving the straight bottom edge open; turn out.

Tip: Cotter pin-joints for bear limbs are attached with a 'key', which looks like a screwdriver but with a fitting at the end that holds the pin, making it easy to turn. Purchase the appropriate key from the joint supplier.

Traditional designs

Big bear *(continued)*

Joints Thread a card ring and then a metal ring on to a pin. Stuff the head firmly, pushing down with a rod. Place the pin and its two rings over the neck opening, pressing firmly to pack down the wadding. Fix the join of the head by pleating the neck fabric all around the pin using thick, strong thread. Knot the threads securely. Make a hole in the top of the body with pointed scissors or an awl to insert the head pin. Thread a card ring then a metal ring on to the pin and use the cotter-pin key to turn each leg of the pin down by rolling it over itself. Join the arms and paws to the body in the same way, then stuff them and close up. Close up the back after stuffing the body.

Face Close up the bottom of the ears, tucking the seam allowances inside, and pin them in place on the head before stitching securely. Mark the location of the eyes with pins. Pierce the fabric with pointed scissors. Using a long tapestry needle and thick thread doubled over, attach each eye as follows: insert the needle at the back of the ear nearest the eye (but do not pull the thread all the way through) and bring it out through the eye hole; thread on the metal ring of the eye and return the needle to the back through the same hole. Pull tightly before knotting the thread ends behind the ear and 'losing' the thread ends under the ear. Embroider the nose and mouth in black.

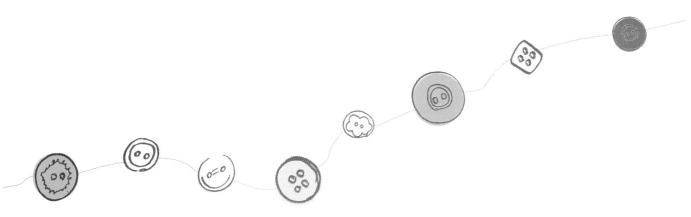

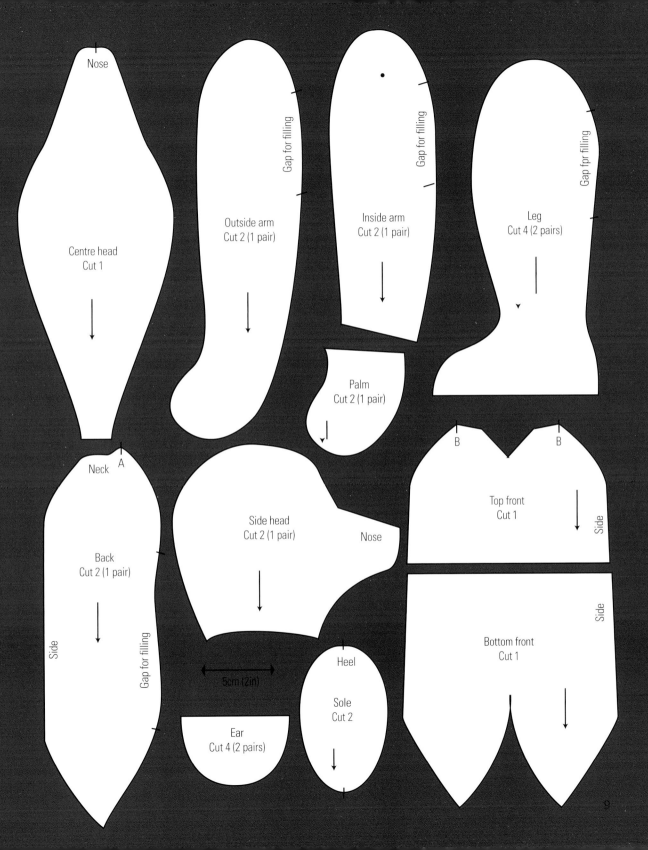

Nose

Centre head
Cut 1

Outside arm
Cut 2 (1 pair)

Gap for filling

Inside arm
Cut 2 (1 pair)

Gap for filling

Leg
Cut 4 (2 pairs)

Gap fpr filling

Palm
Cut 2 (1 pair)

Neck

A

Back
Cut 2 (1 pair)

Side

Gap for filling

Side head
Cut 2 (1 pair)

Nose

5cm (2in)

Ear
Cut 4 (2 pairs)

Heel

Sole
Cut 2

B

B

Top front
Cut 1

Side

Bottom front
Cut 1

Side

9

Tartan handkerchief rabbit

Materials

Four large pink tartan handkerchiefs and one blue one (or other lightweight closely woven cotton fabrics) ● sewing thread ● thin wadding (batting) ● synthetic stuffing ● brown embroidery cotton and embroidery needle for the eyes and nose

Method

Enlarge the patterns on pages 12–13 to size (see page 2). Cut out the following pieces, adding 1cm (⅜in) all round for seam allowances. From the pink handkerchiefs cut two side heads, one centre head, one chin, one tummy, two back pieces, one bottom, two legs, two ears, two tails and two feet. From the blue handkerchief cut two ears and two soles, and from wadding cut four ears. The handkerchiefs do not have a right or wrong side so there is no need to flip the patterns to cut out the symmetrical pairs (arms and ears, for example) although if you use a different fabric you will need to consider this. When joining the pieces, stitch the seams 1cm (⅜in) from the edges with right sides facing.

Body Stitch the tummy between the two back pieces. Close up the curved back seam and then stitch the body around the bottom; turn out through the neck end and stuff. Put aside, leaving the neck open.

Head Stitch the centre head to a side-head piece, starting at the tip of the nose. Repeat on the other side of the top of the head. Stitch the chin between the two side-head pieces beneath the nose; turn out. Embroider the eyes and nose then stuff the head. Sew to the body using small slipstitches. Lay out one blue ear and on top place one pink ear and then two wadding ears. Stitch the edges, leaving the straight edge open. Trim the seam allowances and then turn out. Turn in the seam allowances at the open edge and sew the ears in place.

Arms and legs Join the two parts of each arm, leaving the top (straight edge) open; turn out and stuff. Join the straight edge of a foot (ankle) to the top of each leg. Stitch the rounded part of the foot around the sole (the straight edge becomes part of the back-leg seam). Fold the leg in half and stitch the long back seam; turn out and stuff. Turn in the seam allowances in at the top of the arms and legs. Sew to the body.

Tail Sew the two tail pieces together around the curved edge, turn out, stuff and attach to the body.

Neck bow Cut two strips of blue handkerchief fabric and stitch together along the long edges; turn out and close up the ends. Tie around the neck.

Tartan handkerchief rabbit *(continued)*

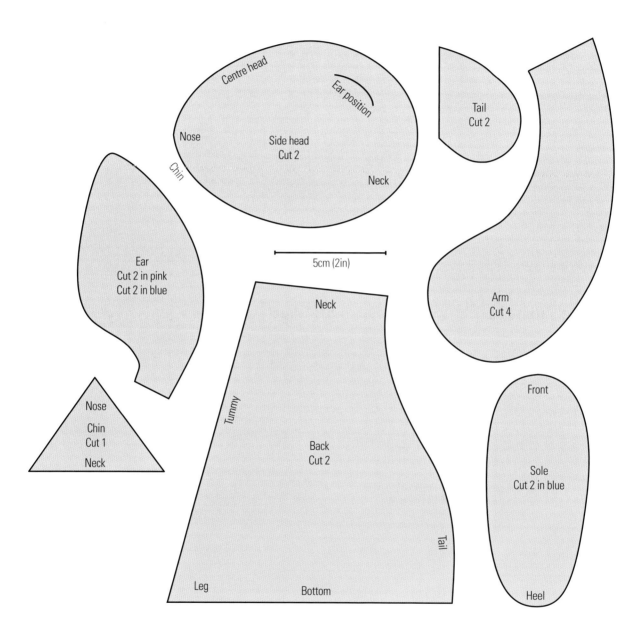

Centre head

Ear position

Nose

Side head
Cut 2

Chin

Neck

Tail
Cut 2

Ear
Cut 2 in pink
Cut 2 in blue

5cm (2in)

Arm
Cut 4

Nose

Chin
Cut 1

Neck

Neck

Tummy

Back
Cut 2

Tail

Front

Sole
Cut 2 in blue

Leg

Bottom

Heel

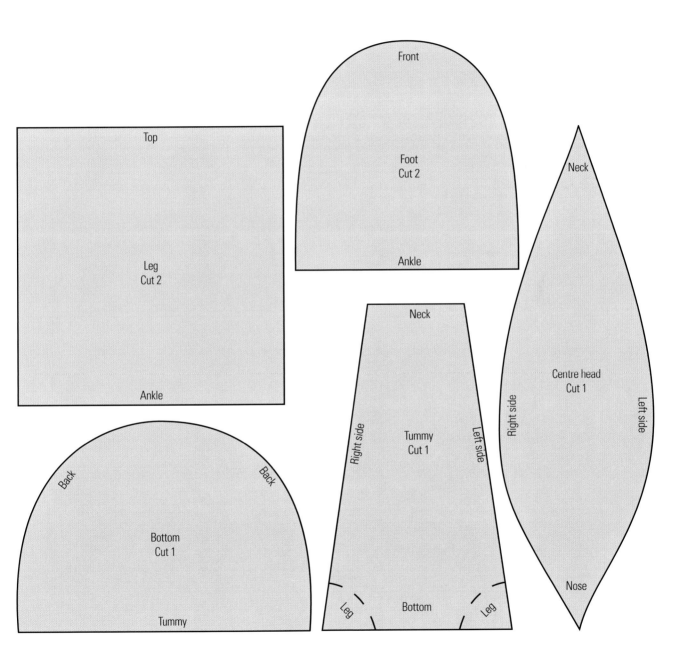

Top

Leg
Cut 2

Ankle

Front

Foot
Cut 2

Ankle

Neck

Centre head
Cut 1

Right side

Left side

Nose

Back

Back

Bottom
Cut 1

Tummy

Neck

Right side

Left side

Tummy
Cut 1

Leg

Bottom

Leg

Mr and Mrs Bear

Materials

For the body of each bear:

60cm (¾yd) ecru cotton fabric ● two black buttons for eyes ● pink embroidery cotton ● synthetic stuffing

For the clothing:

Printed cotton fabrics ● about 1.5m (1½yd) lace for the dress ● 1m (1yd) fine ribbon ● elastic thread for the trousers ● two buttons for the waistcoat

Method

Enlarge the patterns on pages 16–17 to size. Pin them to the wrong side of the fabric and then cut out, adding 1cm (⅜in) all the way round for seam allowances.

Arms and legs Stitch the arms and legs together in pairs with right sides facing. Snip into the seam allowances at curves for ease and then turn out and stuff. Tuck in the seam allowances at the top of each leg and flatten the seam before stitching closed. Close up the top of the arms in the same way.

Head Join the two side-head pieces from A to B. Close up the muzzle from C to C. Close up the darts on the back head. Stitch the ears together in pairs around the curved edge with right sides facing; turn out. Join the side-head and back-head pieces, taking up the ears in the stitching.

Assembly Stitch the bottom piece to the lower edge of the back around the matching curved edge. Join the back and front at the shoulders (sloping sections). Pin the arms and legs in place. Stitch the bottom of the body, one side and the top of the other side. Stitch the head to the neck hole then turn out. Stuff the head and body through the side opening. Close up the gap. Embroider the mouth and nose (see the photograph) and attach the buttons for the eyes.

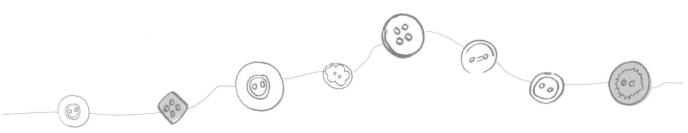

Traditional designs

Mr and Mrs Bear
(*continued*)

Trousers Fold each trouser piece lengthways and close up the inside-leg seam. Place one leg inside the other with right sides facing and stitch the front and back seams. Turn out and hem the top and bottom edges. Slip some elastic thread into the waist hem and tie the ends together to fit the bear. Topstitch the bottom hems, if desired.

Dress Join the back and front dress bodice pieces at the shoulders. Finish the neckline with bias binding cut from the remnants. Attach the sleeves to the armholes. Stitch each underarm sleeve seam and adjacent side seam in one go. Gather the cuffs. For the skirt, cut out a 75 × 20cm (29½ × 8in) rectangle. Join into a ring then hem the bottom edge. Attach the lace to the bottom edge. Gather the top and join to the bodice. Put the dress on the bear and close up the back bodice. Pleat more lace and stitch ribbon down the centre (see the photograph). Tie the pleated lace around the neck. Attach a small ribbon bow to one ear as a finishing touch for Mrs Bear.

Shirt Join the shirt back and front at the shoulders and then attach the sleeves to the armholes. Stitch each underarm

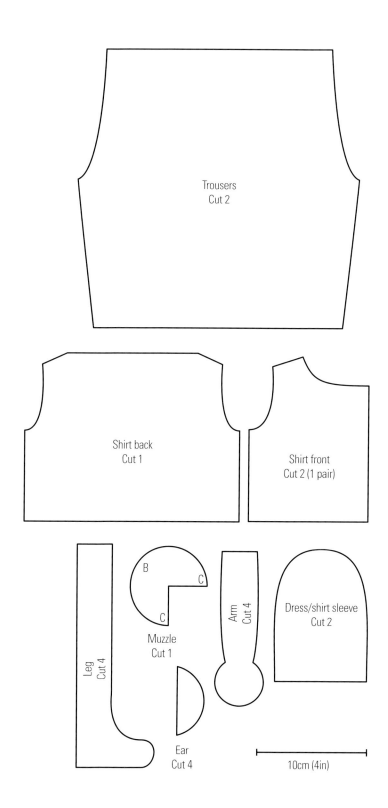

sleeve seam and adjacent side seam in one go. Hem the sleeves, the front edges and the bottom. For the collar, cut out a rectangle 8cm (3in) wide and the length of the neck edge. Fold in half with right sides facing, and close up the ends; turn out. Stitch to the neck. The shirt is held in place by the waistcoat on top.

Waistcoat Join the back to one front at each side. Overlay a second front piece over each attached front with right sides facing. Stitch the curving neck edge, front and bottom edges then turn out. Join the back and front pieces at the shoulders. Slipstitch the inside side-seam edges and hem the remaining raw edges. Close up with two buttons at the front.

Bow tie Join a 15 × 6cm (6 × 2½in) rectangle into a ring. Flatten, placing the seam in the centre of the bottom layer. Stitch the two raw edges, leaving a gap to turn through; turn out and close up the gap. Gather in the middle with a tie in the same fabric.

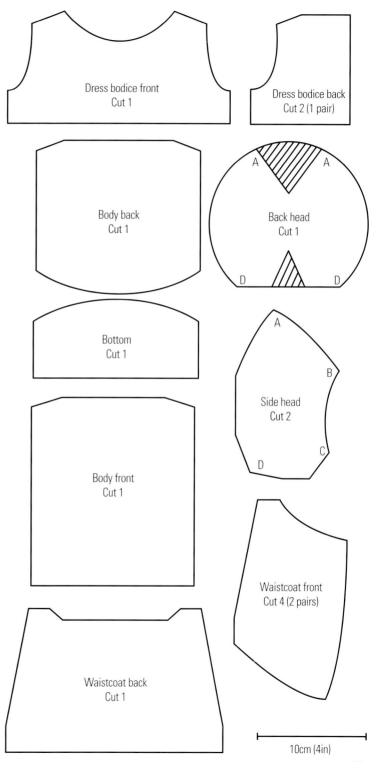

Cuddly bear quilt

Dimensions

Approximately 100 × 70cm (39½ × 27½in)

Materials

1.50m (1¾yd) hemp/natural linen ● 1m (1yd) dotty woollen fabric ● 1m (1yd) tartan woollen fabric ● 2kg (4½lb) stuffing ● two large buttons for the eyes ● linen (or nettle or hemp) thread ● brown tapestry wool and needle ● matching sewing thread

Method

Enlarge all the patterns on pages 20–21 to size (see page 2) and cut them out to obtain the patterns. Cut out the pieces from the fabrics the number of times given on the pattern pieces, cutting from folded fabric to get matched pairs. When joining the pieces, stitch all seams with right sides facing, taking a 1cm (⅜in) seam allowance. Seam allowances are included in the patterns.

Tail, limbs and body Stitch the two pieces of the tail together around the curved edge, snip into the seam allowances for ease and turn out. Join the two back pieces together along the centre-back seam. Join the front paws together in pairs around the curved edges and then repeat for the back paws, mixing the fabrics. Snip into the seam allowances for ease and turn out. Fill the four paws with stuffing. Tack the paws and the tail to the back piece with right sides facing, at the places indicated on the patterns. Tack, then stitch the tummy and back together, taking up the legs and tail between the two pieces and leaving the straight neck edge of the body open; turn out through the gap. Fill the body with stuffing without pressing down so that the bear remains soft.

Head Join the side-head pieces from the tip of the nose at C to the neck at A. Stitch the side-head pieces to the centre-head piece from C to B; turn out and stuff. Stitch the ears together in pairs around the curved edge, turn out and stuff lightly. Fold in the seam allowances along the straight edge, close up and sew the ears to each side of the head, forming a fold to shape the ears slightly. Embroider the nose and mouth with the brown wool. Attach the buttons for eyes. Join the head and body with invisible stitches, folding the seam allowances inside. Sew the patch and pocket on the back using blanket stitch and the linen thread.

Tip: Make your quilt even cuddlier by using fake-fur fabric for the paws and body, with cotton or suedette for the ears and patches.

Cuddly bear quilt *(continued)*

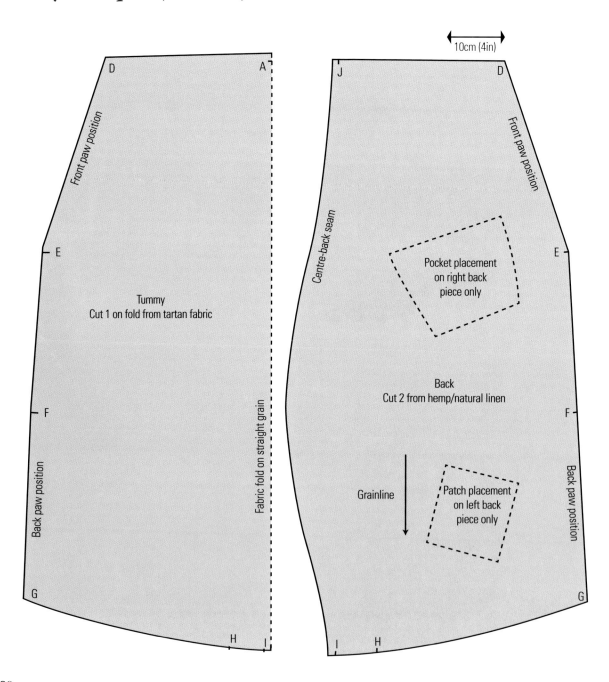

10cm (4in)

D   A

Front paw position

E

Tummy
Cut 1 on fold from tartan fabric

F

Back paw position

Fabric fold on straight grain

G   H   I

J   D

Front paw position

Centre-back seam

E

Pocket placement
on right back
piece only

Back
Cut 2 from hemp/natural linen

F

Grainline

Patch placement
on left back
piece only

Back paw position

I   H   G

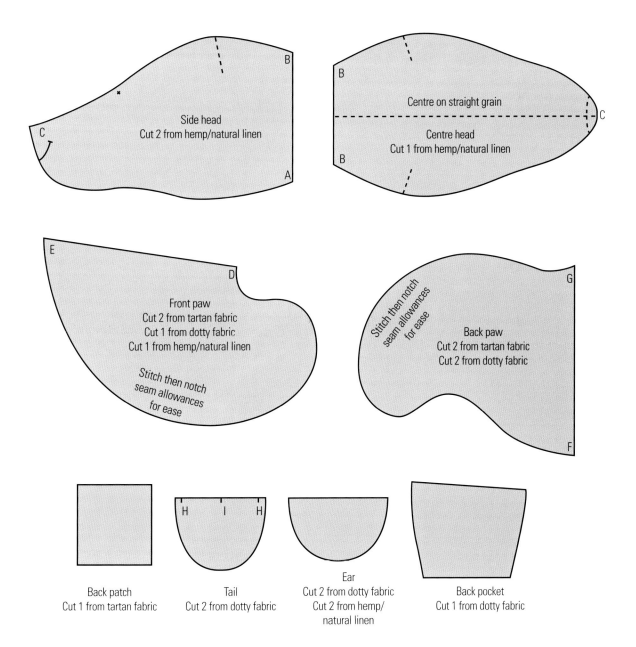

Side head
Cut 2 from hemp/natural linen

B

C

A

B

B

Centre on straight grain

Centre head
Cut 1 from hemp/natural linen

C

E

D

Front paw
Cut 2 from tartan fabric
Cut 1 from dotty fabric
Cut 1 from hemp/natural linen

*Stitch then notch
seam allowances
for ease*

G

*Stitch then notch
seam allowances
for ease*

Back paw
Cut 2 from tartan fabric
Cut 2 from dotty fabric

F

Back patch
Cut 1 from tartan fabric

H I H

Tail
Cut 2 from dotty fabric

Ear
Cut 2 from dotty fabric
Cut 2 from hemp/
natural linen

Back pocket
Cut 1 from dotty fabric

Gingham bear

Materials

Old dishcloths ● red-and-white gingham ● red embroidery cotton and embroidery needle ● white sewing thread ● synthetic stuffing

Method

Enlarge the shapes of the pieces from pages 24–25 (see page 2) and cut out from fabric, mixing cloth fabrics and gingham. Cut out, adding 5mm (¼in) all round for seam allowances. When cutting the arms, cut two full arms for the outside-arm pieces. Cut (or fold) the pattern along the broken line and cut two paws and two inner arms, remembering to add seam allowances all round, even along the edge of the broken line. Whip all the edges to prevent fraying. When joining the pieces, stitch them together with right sides facing, taking a 5mm (¼in) seam allowance.

Head Stitch the ears together in pairs around the curved edge and turn out. Slip them into the darts on the side-head pieces and stitch in place. Flatten the ears towards the front and tack down out of the way. Stitch the centre head between the two side-head pieces from nose to nape of neck; turn out. Stitch the side-head pieces together from nose to front-neck edge.

Body Stitch the two parts of the back together, leaving a gap in the middle for stuffing. Stitch the two parts of the front together. Join the back to the front and turn out through the gap in the centre back.

Arms and legs Sew a paw to each inside arm. Stitch each inside arm to an outside arm, leaving a gap to turn out the pieces. Turn the arms right sides out. Stitch the legs together in pairs, leaving the bottom edge open and a gap in the back of the leg to turn the pieces out. Attach the sole and turn out the legs.

Assembly Fill all the pieces with stuffing and close up the gaps. Sew the head to the body. Attach the arms and legs to the body with double ties in red thread. Embroider the eyes and nose with straight stitches.

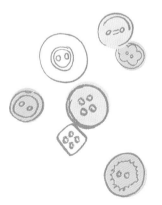

Gingham bear *(continued)*

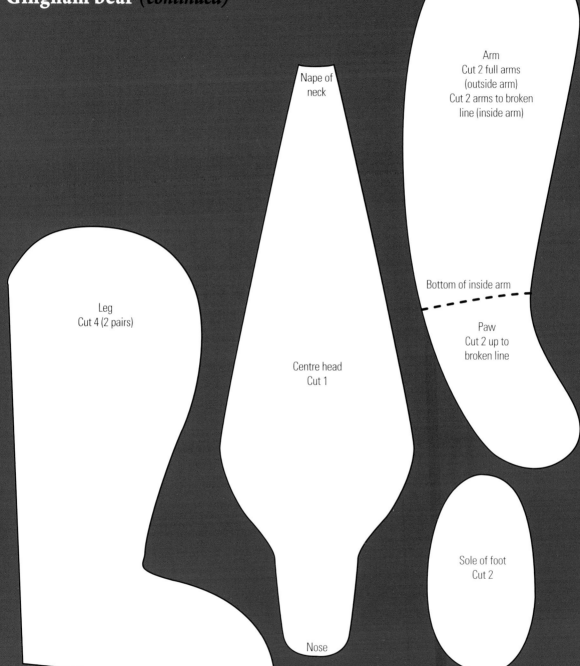

Nape of
neck

Arm
Cut 2 full arms
(outside arm)
Cut 2 arms to broken
line (inside arm)

Leg
Cut 4 (2 pairs)

Bottom of inside arm

Paw
Cut 2 up to
broken line

Centre head
Cut 1

Sole of foot
Cut 2

Nose

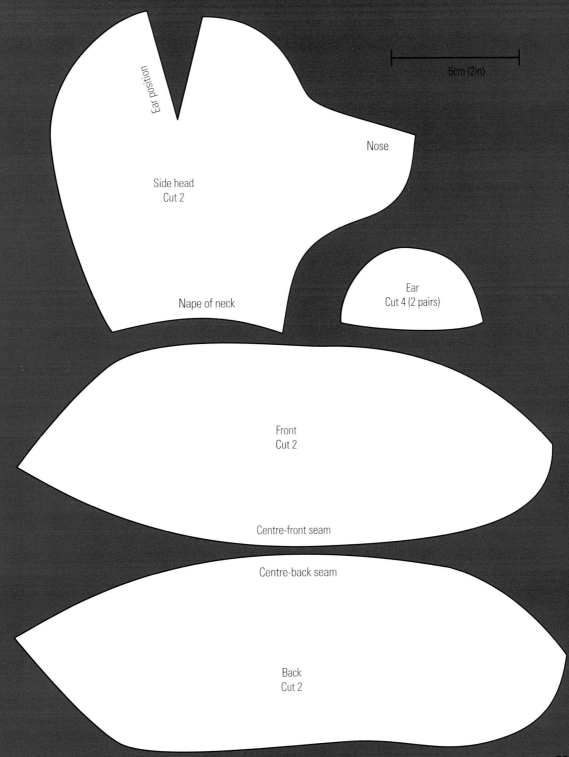

Ear position

Nose

Side head
Cut 2

5cm (2in)

Ear
Cut 4 (2 pairs)

Nape of neck

Front
Cut 2

Centre-front seam

Centre-back seam

Back
Cut 2

25

Three bear cushions

Dimensions

30cm (12in) diameter

Materials

Three round 30cm (12in) cushion pads ● 35cm (½yd) velvet for each cushion ● fabric remnants for the noses and inner ears (velvet/tweed/woollen fabrics etc.) ● embroidery cotton for the mouths and eyes ● thread to match the fabric ● stuffing to pad the muzzle, nose and ears of each bear

Method

For each cushion, cut out two 35cm (14in) diameter circles from the velvet (includes seam allowances). Trace the patterns on pages 28–29 and cut out to make the patterns. From the remnants cut one muzzle, two pairs of ears (in velvet) plus two inner ears and one nose, adding 5mm (¼in) extra all round for seam allowances.

Muzzle and nose Using the appliqué technique, sew the muzzle to the right side of one of the velvet circles using small, hidden stitches and tucking the seam allowance under as you sew. Leave a gap for stuffing. Slip a little stuffing inside and then close the gap. Attach the nose to the muzzle in the same way.

Ears and mouth Attach each inner ear to one velvet ear around the curved edge using the appliqué technique, then sew this ear to a plain velvet ear with right sides facing, leaving the bottom edge open. Turn out and fill with a little stuffing. Tack the ears in place on the front of the head, matching the raw edges. Embroider a mouth in backstitch and the eyes with large straight stitches.

Assembly Stitch the two velvet circles right sides together, 2cm (¾in) from the edges, leaving a gap. Cut notches in the seam allowances for ease then turn right sides out. Slip the cushion pad into the cover and close up the gap with small stitches.

Tip: It is a little fiddly tacking the ears to the head because of the curves. It helps if you snip into the seam allowance of the ears for ease, being careful not to snip over the stitching line.

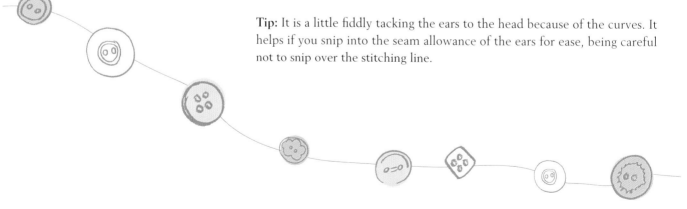

Nose
Cut 1

Muzzle
Cut 1
Embroider the mouth and appliqué the nose

5cm (2in)

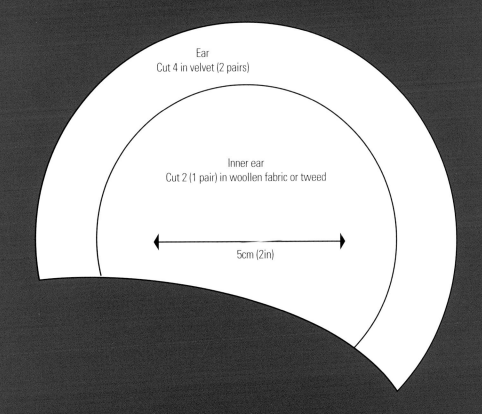

Ear
Cut 4 in velvet (2 pairs)

Inner ear
Cut 2 (1 pair) in woollen fabric or tweed

5cm (2in)

Chef bear

Dimensions

About 40cm (16in)

Materials

For the bear:
40cm (½yd) beige linen ● 10cm (4in) white linen ● 10cm (4in) fusible interfacing ● white sewing thread ● DMC stranded embroidery cotton in red 321 and brown 839 ● synthetic stuffing

For the clothing:
Striped dishcloth in red and white ● 40cm (½yd) white linen ● 40cm (½yd) red gingham ● three mother-of-pearl buttons ● 40cm (½yd) flat elastic, 1cm (⅜in) wide ● white sewing thread

Method

Enlarge the bear and clothing patterns on pages 32–33 using a photocopier (see page 2). Cut out to obtain the patterns. Fuse the interfacing to the white linen for the body. Fold the fabrics in half with right sides facing and pin the patterns on top. Cut out the following, adding 0.5cm (¼in) all round the bear pieces and 1cm (⅜in) around the clothes:

- From beige linen: two side-head pieces, one centre head, two ears, two arms, two legs and two bodies.
- From the interfaced white linen: one muzzle, two soles and two ears.

Head Stitch each white ear to a beige ear, right sides facing, leaving a gap at the base; turn out and press. Fold the ears in half, white on the inside, and tack in position on the centre-head piece (the ears will be stitched in the seam when the side-head pieces are attached). Close up the dart on the side-head pieces and then stitch to the centre-head piece with right sides facing, starting at the nape of the neck. Fold the muzzle in half and sew to the front of the head. Close up the bottom of the muzzle and then the front neck in the extension; turn out and press. Fill the muzzle with stuffing. Whip on each side to contain the stuffing. Embroider the nose in red and the eyes in brown. Stuff the rest of the head.

Arms and legs Fold the arms in half. Stitch the seam around the paw to the top of each arm. Turn out and stuff to within 1.5cm (⅝in) of the open end. Close up the top horizontally. Fold each leg in half and stitch the side seam then insert the sole. Turn out and stuff to within 1.5cm (⅝in) of the top edge; close up the top.

Body Place the two parts of the body together with right sides facing. Put the arms and legs into place. Stitch the edges of the body, leaving the top open and catching the limbs in the seam; turn out and stuff. Place the head on the body and join with secure, double-thread stitching.

Cutting the clothes From the white linen cut two jacket fronts and the back (pinning the pattern on the fold of the fabric); from the dishcloth cut two trouser legs, placing the bottom on the stripes; from the gingham cut one scarf

Chef bear (*continued*)

using the measurements on the diagram, without adding a seam allowance. Cut linings for the jacket and trousers from the same or different fabrics.

Chef's jacket Make a linen jacket and a lining separately, joining backs and fronts at the shoulders and bottoms of arms with right sides facing. Turn the jacket wrong side out then pin the edges of the fronts and back neck to the lining with right sides together. The sleeves hang outside. Stitch together, leaving the bottom of the back open to turn through. Leaving the jackets on the wrong side, put together the cuff of a lining and linen sleeve to stitch the edges right sides together. Turn the jackets, slip the lining jacket inside and slip each lining sleeve into the linen one. Turn a 3cm (1¼in) cuff. Iron, marking the fold of the

collar. Embroider three buttonholes at regular intervals then attach buttons to the opposite edge to correspond.
Trousers Make a pair of dishcloth trousers and a pair of trouser linings separately: fold each piece lengthways and stitch the inside leg seams then slip one leg inside the other, right sides facing, to stitch the front and back seams in one go. Slip the two pairs of trousers one inside the other, right sides facing. Stitch the bottom of the legs; turn. Turn the lining trousers inside. Make a hem fold of 1cm (⅜in) then 1.5cm (⅝in) at waist level; stitch, leaving a gap. Slip in the elastic and join in a ring. Close up the gap.
Scarf Neaten the edges then make a little hem fold of 0.5cm (¼in) with an iron all the way round and stitch in place.

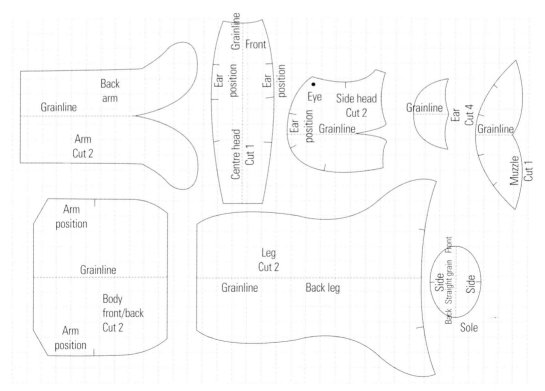

1 square = 2 × 2cm (¾ × ¾in)

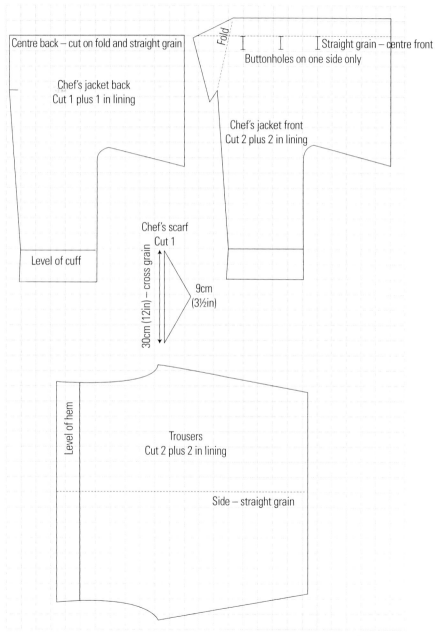

Centre back – cut on fold and straight grain

Chef's jacket back
Cut 1 plus 1 in lining

Level of cuff

Fold

Straight grain – centre front
Buttonholes on one side only

Chef's jacket front
Cut 2 plus 2 in lining

Chef's scarf
Cut 1

30cm (12in) – cross grain

9cm
(3½in)

Level of hem

Trousers
Cut 2 plus 2 in lining

Side – straight grain

1 square = 2 × 2cm (¾ × ¾in)

Christmas-tree bird

Dimensions

Approximately 16cm (6¼in)

Materials

For each bird:
20cm (8in) square in each of two purple cotton fabrics ● synthetic stuffing ● violet ribbons and lace ● violet and off-white satin ribbon ● lace motifs ● mini violet tassel ● two mini violet pompons ● two beads for the eyes ● decorative bead ● matching sewing thread ● matching embroidery cotton

Method

Enlarge the pattern of the body and wing to size (see page 2). From the first fabric cut one body and two wings; cut the same pieces again from the other fabric, this time flipping the patterns over to make a symmetrical pair. Stitch the two bodies together with right sides facing, leaving a gap under the tummy; turn out and stuff. Close up the gap with small hand stitches. Repeat with the wings. Sew a wing on to each side of the body.

Finishing Embroider a strong bar on the back so you can thread on a ribbon for hanging. Cover the beak with straight stitches. Sew on the beads for the eyes and attach a ribbon around the neck, decorated with a lace motif. Sew the tassel and pompons to the ribbons or lace to hang under the body after threading on the decorative bead.

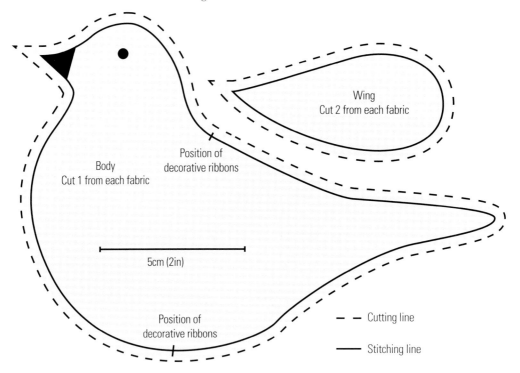

Wing
Cut 2 from each fabric

Position of
decorative ribbons

Body
Cut 1 from each fabric

5cm (2in)

Position of
decorative ribbons

- - - Cutting line

——— Stitching line

Animal cushions

Materials

For each cushion:

1m (1yd) cotton fabric for the base (body) plus assorted remnants (ears, beak and muzzle etc.) ● 1m (1yd) wadding (batting) fabric for the sheep only ● polyester foam to fill the cushions ● two buttons for the eyes ● DMC stranded embroidery cotton ● matching sewing thread ● pipe cleaner for the pig's tail ● cord for the cow's tail

Method

Sheep cushion Enlarge the pattern to size and cut out (see page 2). Fold the base fabric in half, right sides facing, and cut out the entire sheep twice, adding 1cm (⅜in) all round for seams. Cut out the body from the wadding fabric also, folded in half. Pin a wadding body to the wrong side of each fabric body. Embroider the scallops, which suggest the sheep's fleece, in running stitch using embroidery cotton. Cut out the fabric for the head and feet, adding 1cm (⅜in) all round; pin in place. Fold the seam allowance at the top of the feet and back of the head to the wrong side and sew to the body with overcast stitching. Place the two bodies together with right sides facing and stitch the edges, leaving a gap to turn through. Snip the seam allowances for ease then turn out and fill with foam. Close up the gap by hand. Cut out four fabric ears and two wadding ears, adding seam allowances. Place the fabric ears together in pairs with right sides facing and add a wadding ear on top then stitch the edges, leaving the bottom (where the ear joins the face) open. Snip the seam allowances for ease and turn out. Close up the bottom of each ear by hand, tucking the seam allowances inside. Sew the ears in place then attach the buttons for the eyes.

5cm (2in)

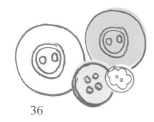

Animal cushions *(continued)*

Pig, rabbit, cow and goose cushions Enlarge the patterns and cut out. Cut out the bodies from the base fabric, folded right sides together, adding 1 cm (⅜in) all round for seams. Cut out the remaining shapes from the other fabrics, adding 1 cm (⅜in) seam allowances – note that some of the patches extend over to the other side of the animals and should be cut accordingly. Attach the nose of the cow or rabbit and the beak and feet of the goose using overcast stitch and tucking the seam allowances under. Place the two body shapes together with right sides facing and stitch the edges, leaving a gap to turn through. Snip the seam allowances for ease then turn out and stuff the animal. Close up the gap by hand. Iron a little turning to the wrong side around each patch then sew in position using different embroidery stitches across the edges. Make the ears for the pig and cow as described for the sheep (see above) then sew in position. Sew on the buttons for the eyes. The pig's tail is made using a piece of fabric sewn around a pipe cleaner, the cow's tail is a piece of fabric sewn around a thin cord and fringed at the end. Embroider the rabbit's whiskers with black backstitch and the curve of the legs with thread to match the fabric.

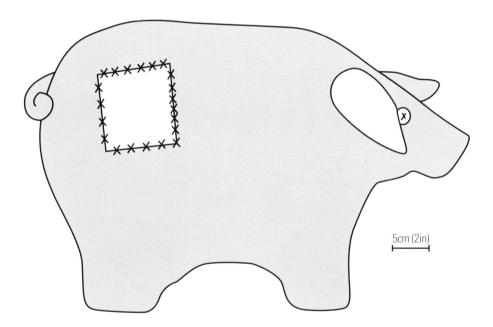

5cm (2in)

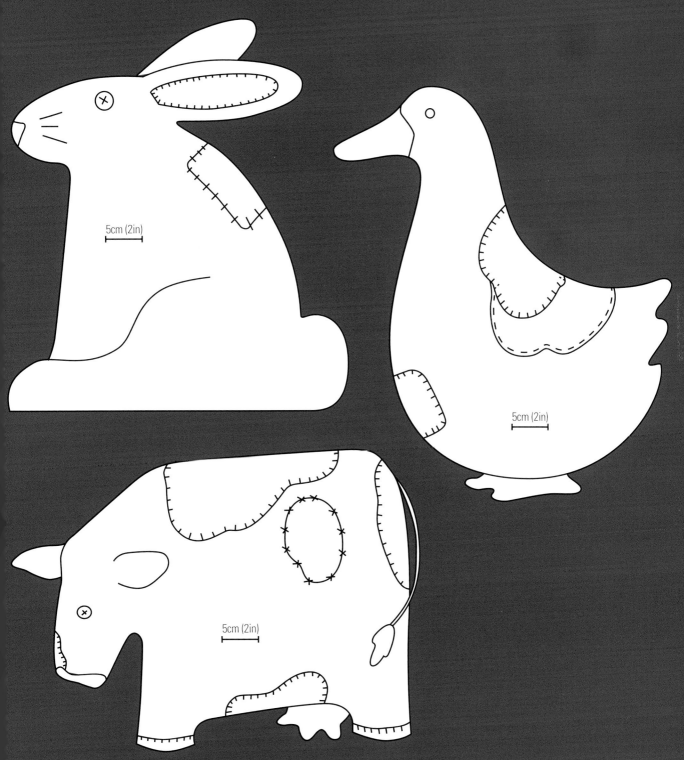

5cm (2in)

5cm (2in)

5cm (2in)

Giant bear

Dimensions

Height about 1m (40in)

Materials

Two old large canvas fertiliser sacks (or 2m/2yd coarse canvas) ● 3kg (6½lb) kapok (or other soft stuffing) ● two large buttons for the eyes ● brown wool and needle to embroider the mouth ● strong linen thread ● matching sewing thread ● 20cm (8in) mattress needle ● dressmakers' squared paper

Method

Copy the parts of the pattern from pages 42–43 on to the squared paper, enlarging it to size. Cut out each part to obtain the pattern. Fold the canvas in half and pin the templates on top. Cut out, adding 1cm (⅜in) all the way round for seam allowances. When joining pieces, stitch them together with right sides facing, 1cm (⅜in) from the edges.

Head Stitch the darts on the side-head pieces, after folding the fabric right sides together. Join the side-head pieces to the centre-head piece from nose (B) to nape of neck (A). Stitch the side-head pieces together from the nose to the front neck edge; turn out the head and stuff with kapok. Close up, gathering the neck with the strong linen thread. Fold the seam allowances to the wrong side around the nose and stitch to the head with the linen thread. Sew on the buttons for the eyes. Embroider the mouth with the brown wool using running stitch.

Ears Stitch the ears together in pairs around the curved edge, leaving the base open; snip into the seam allowances for ease then turn out and stuff lightly. Close up the base, folding the seam allowances inside. Sew the ears to the head, folding to form a 90° angle.

Body Close up the dart at the lower edge of each body piece. Join the two body parts, leaving the neck open; turn out and stuff. Close up, gathering the neck with the strong linen thread.

Legs Stitch the legs together in pairs, leaving the foot open between A and B and a gap in the back seam for stuffing. Stitch a sole into the bottom of each leg, aligning the reference points. Snip into the seam allowances for ease then turn out the legs and stuff them. Close up the gaps with linen thread.

Arms Stitch the arms together in pairs, leaving a gap in the back seam for stuffing. Snip into the seam allowances for ease then turn out the arms and stuff them. Close up the gaps with linen thread.

Joints Using the linen thread, join the body and head securely, then join the arms to the body, crossing the body at shoulder level, using the mattress needle and linen thread. Finally, join the legs to the body, crossing the body at hip level.

Giant bear *(continued)*

Tip: Detailed instructions on how to thread joint a bear can be found on the Internet. When done correctly, the arms and legs will be able to move.

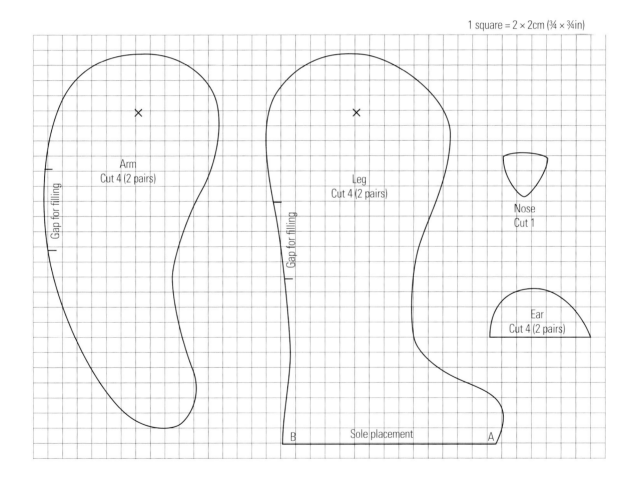

1 square = 2 × 2cm (¾ × ¾in)

Arm
Cut 4 (2 pairs)

Gap for filling

Leg
Cut 4 (2 pairs)

Gap for filling

Nose
Cut 1

Ear
Cut 4 (2 pairs)

B   Sole placement   A

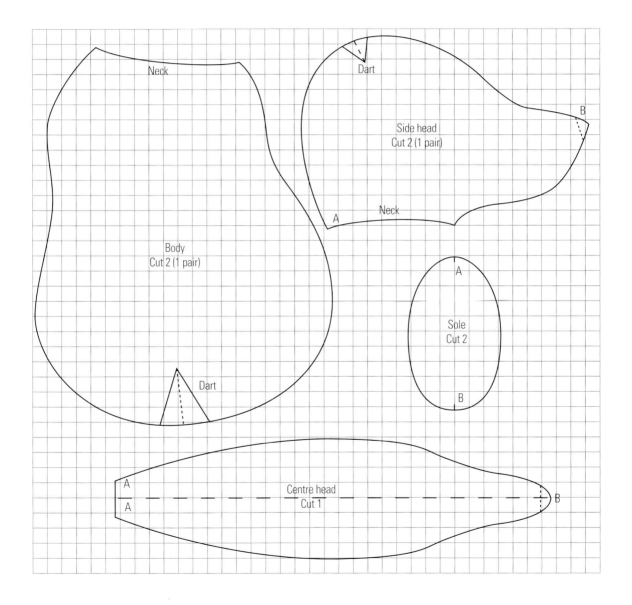

Neck

Dart

Side head
Cut 2 (1 pair)

B

A   Neck

Body
Cut 2 (1 pair)

A

Sole
Cut 2

Dart

B

A
A   Centre head
Cut 1   B

43

bright colours
and fun designs

Bright colours and fun designs

Easter bunnies

Materials

Pair of knitted gloves (wool or cotton) matching sewing thread synthetic stuffing buttons embroidery cotton ribbons cotton fabric remnants little pompom for the tail (optional)

Method

Preparation Turn the gloves inside out. For the body, sew the base of the middle finger and ring finger horizontally, then the base of the thumb vertically (see diagram 1 on page 48). For the head, sew the base of the middle finger horizontally and the base of the thumb and the edge of the little finger vertically. Trim off the excess but save the fingers cut from the body to make the arms and tail.

Head Fold the head piece, overlaying the two remaining fingers as shown in diagram 2 on page 48. Sew a point to shape the nose, then stitch straight down to the base.

Body Turn the body right side out and fill with stuffing. Fill the two middle fingers you removed from the body and head sections to make the arms. Whip the cut edges securely, pull to close up and tie. Shorten the other removed finger and fill to make the tail or use a pompom.

Assembly Turn the head right side out and fill with stuffing. Sew the arms and tail in place on the body. Slide the neck into the top of the body and sew securely (see diagram 3 on page 49). Sew on buttons for the eyes, nose and belly button then use embroidery to add other embellishments such as the whiskers. Tie a ribbon around the neck to finish.

Bright colours and fun designs

(continued)

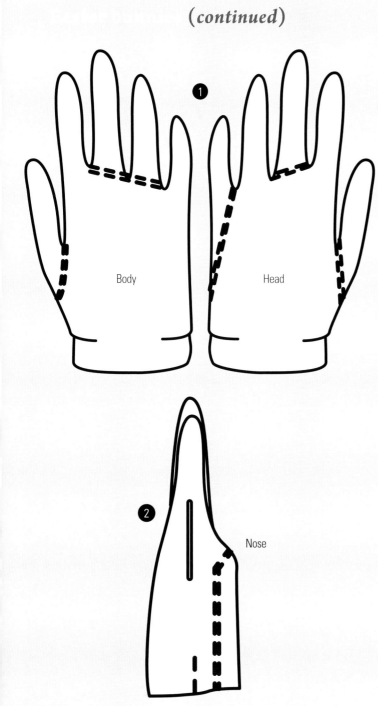

Body

Head

Nose

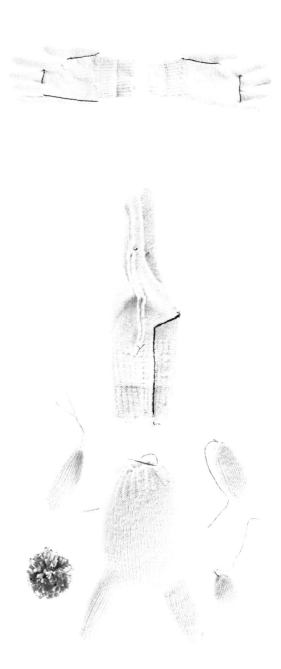

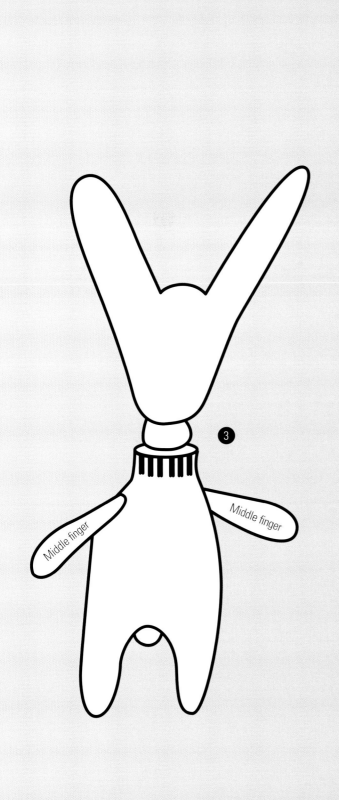

Middle finger

Middle finger

3

Songbird key holders

Finished size

About 15cm (6in) tall

Materials

Woollen and cotton fabric remnants
   matching thread   cord for hanging
   synthetic stuffing

Method

Trace the patterns and cut out. For each bird, cut out two bodies from woollen fabric, adding a small seam allowance all round; cut out the other parts the number of times indicated without adding seam allowances.

Assembly Stitch the wings, legs and beak pieces together in pairs, wrong sides facing, using zigzag stitch all the way round. Attach the eyes and tummy to one body piece, using zigzag stitch around the edges. Stitch the middle of the beak to the head. Mark the pupils with satin stitch. Place the two body pieces together with right sides facing. Position the wings and legs and add a cord loop at the top of the head for the key, noting that the body will be turned out so the wings, feet and cord need to be placed accordingly. Stitch the edges, leaving a gap on the side of the head; turn out and stuff the bird. Close up the gap by hand.

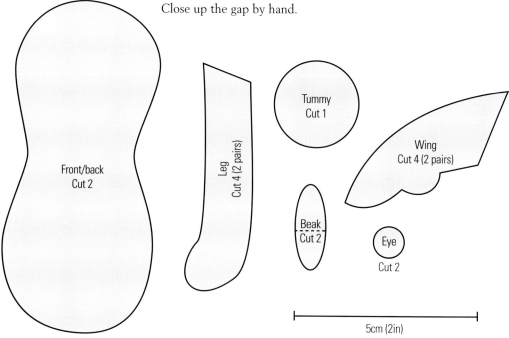

Front/back
Cut 2

Leg
Cut 4 (2 pairs)

Tummy
Cut 1

Beak
Cut 2

Eye
Cut 2

Wing
Cut 4 (2 pairs)

5cm (2in)

Milk-tooth bear

Materials

About 30cm (12in) square each of blue and beige woollen fabric • 6 × 12cm (2⅜ × 4¾in) checked woollen fabric for the tooth pocket • two circles of ecru woollen fabric for the eyes • matching sewing thread • blue pearl cotton, a little darker than the fabric • small button • synthetic stuffing

Method

Cut out the patterns on pages 54–55. From each woollen fabric cut one body, one head, two arms, two legs and two ears, adding 5mm (¼in) seam allowances all round. Cut out the muzzle in beige wool and the eyes in ecru without adding seam allowances. From checked fabric, cut the pocket (A) without adding seam allowances, then cut the two pocket flaps (B), this time adding seam allowances all round. When joining pieces, stitch all the seams with right sides facing, 5mm (¼in) from the edges unless otherwise stated.

Tooth pocket Stitch a 3mm (⅛in) hem at the top of the pocket (A). Sew the button on to the pocket. Position the pocket on the blue body and attach it with satin stitch around the curved the edge. Stitch the flaps of the pocket together with right sides facing, leaving the straight edge open; turn out. Embroider a button bar in the middle of the curve. Place the pocket flap above the pocket, turned upwards; stitch in place then press down.

Head Attach the muzzle and eyes to the blue head by working satin stitch around the edges in matching thread. Embroider the pupils, nose and mouth with blue satin stitch. Stitch the blue head to the blue body and the brown head to the brown body.

Assembly Stitch the arms, legs and ears together in pairs with right sides facing (one blue and one beige in each pair), leaving the straight end open; turn out. Stuff the arms and legs. Place the two sides of the body together with right sides facing. Position the ears, arms and legs so that when turned out they will be sandwiched in place. Stitch the edges, leaving a gap on one side to turn through. Turn the bear out, stuff it and close up the gap.

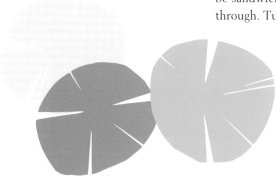

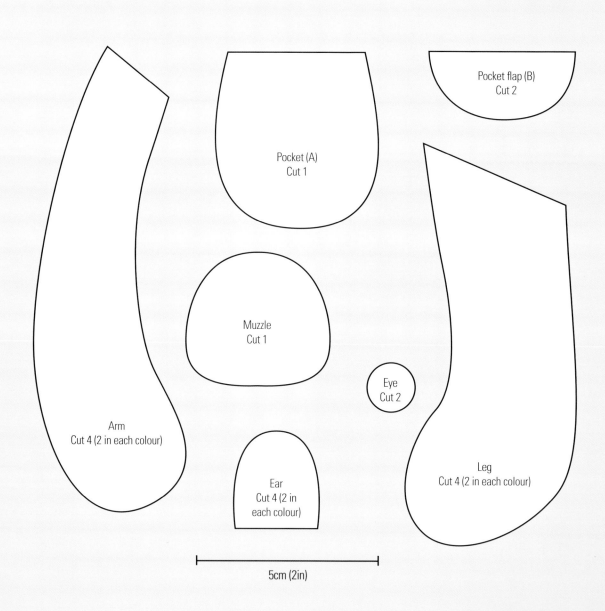

Pocket flap (B)
Cut 2

Pocket (A)
Cut 1

Muzzle
Cut 1

Eye
Cut 2

Arm
Cut 4 (2 in each colour)

Ear
Cut 4 (2 in
each colour)

Leg
Cut 4 (2 in each colour)

5cm (2in)

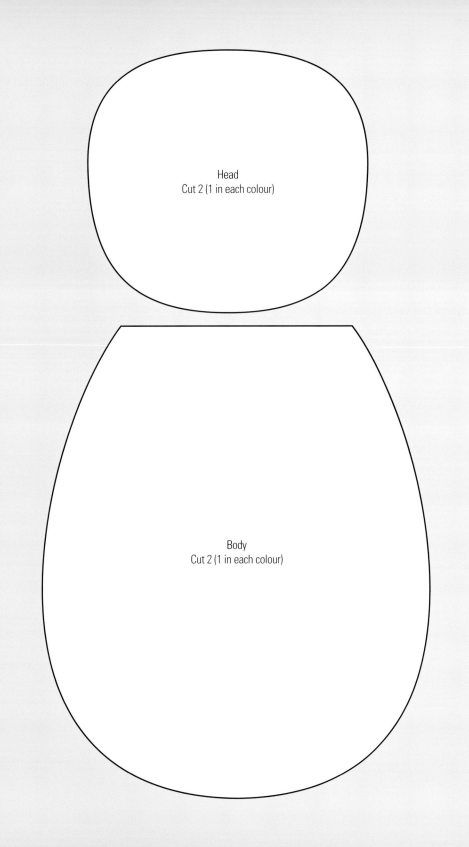

Head
Cut 2 (1 in each colour)

Body
Cut 2 (1 in each colour)

Red giraffe

About 35cm (14in) from the top of the head to the tip of the tail

Cotton fabric remnants in bright red, blue and green ● matching sewing thread ● embroidery cotton in the colours of your choice ● two small silver beads for the pupils ● synthetic stuffing ● a little yellow, red and green yarn or mini pompoms

Method

Trace the diagrams on pages 58–59 and cut out the patterns. Fold the fabrics with right sides together to cut out the pieces. Cut out the head, body and back, adding 1cm (⅜in) seam allowances; when cutting out the mouth, add 5mm (¼in) all round and for the wing, add 1cm (⅜in) to the short straight edge and 5mm (¼in) to the other edges for seams. Cut out one 17 × 7cm (6¾ × 2¾in) red rectangle for the neck; two 9 × 5cm (3½ × 2in) green rectangles for the legs; one red rectangle and one blue rectangle measuring 5 × 6cm (2 × 2⅜in) for the tail; 12 rectangles measuring 3 × 4cm (1¼ × 1½in) for the pompom stalks and toes, and one 40 × 2cm (15¾ × ¾in) strip for the carrying strap. When joining pieces, stitch all seams with right sides together, 1cm (⅜in) from the edges, unless otherwise specified. To prevent the seams puckering, trim the seam allowances before turning out the parts.

Pompom stalks Take one of the 3 × 4cm (1¼ × 1½in) rectangles and roll it over on itself to make a little roll 3cm (1¼in) long. Whip stitch the edge in place. Make a total of six pompom stalks in this way, three for the head and three for the tail. Make six little pompoms from the yarns, ready to sew to the end of each stalk.

Head Stitch the dart in each head piece. Pin three pompom stalks on to the right side of a head piece in the position marked so that the ends of the stalks will be caught in the seam stitching (note how the stalks will sit when the head is turned right side out). Stitch the two head pieces right sides together, leaving a gap for the neck; turn out and stuff but do not close up the gap.

Neck Fold the neck piece in half lengthways and stitch the two 17cm (6¾in) edges right sides together; turn out and stuff.

Body With right sides facing, stitch a front piece to each side of the back from the neck to the base, matching the circles and triangles. Stitch the front seam from the neck edge to the circle, leaving the neck end open. Turn out and stuff the body. Slide the neck into the head then into the body and stitch securely.

Tail Stitch the blue and red rectangles together all round, leaving one 5cm (2in) end open. Turn out the tail, stuff it and close up the gap. Attach the tail to the body, securing three pompon stalks in the seam.

Legs Fold each leg piece in half lengthways with right sides facing and stitch across one end and up the 9cm (3½in) edge; turn out and stuff. Make six toes like the pompom stalks but finishing one end of each in a point. Tuck 5mm (¼in) in at the open end of each leg and attach three toes in a fan shape. Sew the legs to each side of the body.

Wings Cut out 50 × 1.5cm (20 × ½in) bias strips from the red remnants. Iron down a small turning on each long edge then fold in two, wrong sides together. Place one blue wing and one green wing wrong sides together and attach the bias binding all round except on the short straight edge. Slip a little filling inside. Make the second wing in the same way. Tuck in the seam allowance at the open end and attach a wing to each side of the body in the position marked on the body pattern.

Mouth Stitch the two mouth parts together 5mm (¼in) from the edge, leaving a gap in one long side; turn out. Close up the gap. Sew the mouth to the front of the head on the foldline.

Eyes Cut out two blue 2cm (¾in) circles. Tack a small hem all round. Sew one to each side of the head, slipping in a little filling at the bottom. Embroider with large buttonhole stitch all the way round, from the centre to the edge. Sew a silver bead to the centre of each eye.

Embellishment Decorate the head with embroidered stars, using straight stitching then stitch the neck with lines of herringbone stitch and the edges of the neck where it joins the body with a collar in couching chevrons. Cut out an assortment of fabric appliqué decorations and pin them in place. Stitch them down with a couching stitch in a contrasting colour on the edge of the motifs. Attach a pompom to the end of each pompom stalk.

Carrying strap Turn under a small seam allowance on each long edge of the strap piece and then fold wrong sides together. Whip stitch the folded edges together. Attach securely to the back of the head and the top of the tail, folding under the ends.

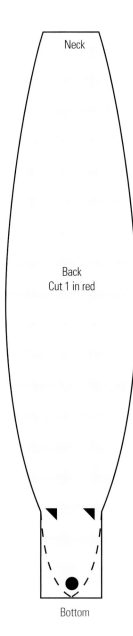

Neck

Back
Cut 1 in red

Bottom

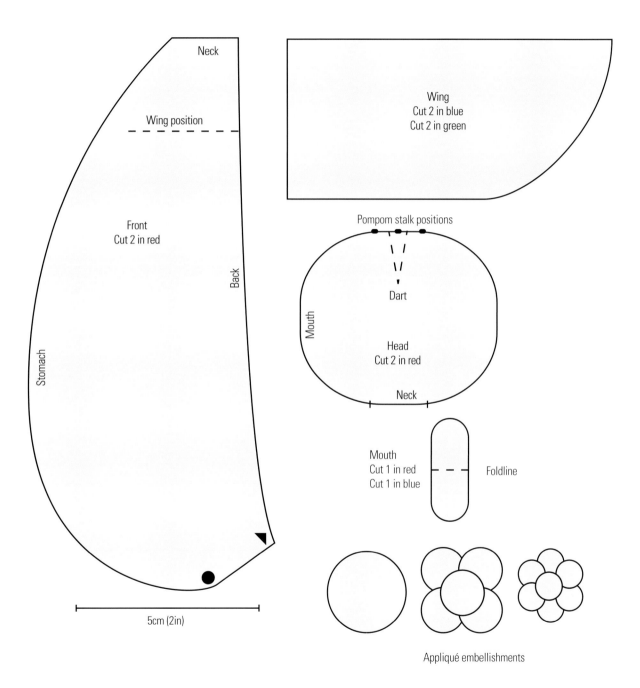

Neck

Wing position

Front
Cut 2 in red

Back

Stomach

5cm (2in)

Wing
Cut 2 in blue
Cut 2 in green

Pompom stalk positions

Dart

Mouth

Head
Cut 2 in red

Neck

Mouth
Cut 1 in red
Cut 1 in blue

Foldline

Appliqué embellishments

Bright colours and fun designs

Boxy bunnies

Materials

Fabric remnants   fabric marker pen   pink fabric paint stick or pink acrylic paint   embroidery cotton   synthetic stuffing   embellishments of your choice such as lace, buttons and ribbons   white felt pen to add a message (or the colour of your choice)   old newspaper   acrylic paints   clear wax   little boxes   ribbon, cord or string to attach the label   card or thin cardboard to make a label   paper glue   brooch pin and felt or wool remnant for a brooch bunny

Method

Enlarge the patterns to the size you like and cut out. Fold your fabric (old knitting, felt, wool or cotton, for example) in half with wrong sides facing and trace the body outlines. Stitch 4mm (⅛in) inside the edges, leaving a gap. Cut out on the line. Fill with a little stuffing and close up the gap. Oversew the edges of each piece with fancy thread. Repeat to make two arms and two legs. Mark the claws with large straight stitches. Sew the legs and arms to the body with large stitches.

Personalising the rabbit Embroider the eyes and nose with satin stitch and the mouth with straight stitches. Use lengths of thread for whiskers, attaching them to the body with a backstitch or knot. Colour the cheeks with the paint stick or use pink acrylic paint. Add lace, ribbons, buttons and other embellishments, fixed with small stitches. Make other rabbits, perhaps in different sizes and colours as desired.

Presentation Cut out a cardboard rectangle for a label and paint it in a background colour. When dry, write a suitable message such as 'Happy birthday' or 'Happy New Year' using a felt pen. Make holes in the card and thread through a cord, ribbon or string to fix the label in place. Present the rabbits in little boxes, perhaps covered with old newspaper then finished with weak paint and clear wax. If desired, you can attach a cord loop to the back of the box so it can be hung up on a wall or Christmas tree.

Brooch To make a brooch bunny, make a rabbit as described above but only using the top part of the pattern and without arms or legs, and add a strip of felt or woollen fabric to the bottom. Sew a brooch pin to the back.

Tip: Reduce the size of the patterns on a photocopier to make baby rabbits in different colours. These could be hung on keychains or used as dangles on bags. You could also fill the bodies with lavender instead of stuffing to pop in a drawer.

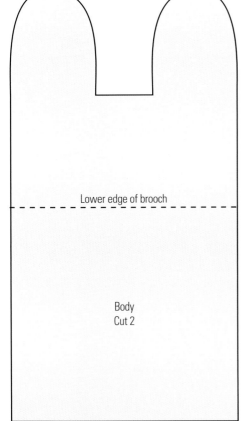

Lower edge of brooch

Body
Cut 2

Arm
Cut 4

Leg
Cut 4

Bear wallet

Dimensions

About 16cm (6¼in) tall

Materials

Coordinating woollen and cotton fabrics ▪ sewing thread ▪ blue and brown pearl cotton ▪ three buttons ▪ fine cord

Method

Copy the patterns from pages 64–65. Cut out the pieces from woollen or cotton fabrics the number of times indicated, adding 5mm (¼in) around each one and folding the fabric before cutting the arms and legs to make sure you have two pairs of each. When joining pieces, stitch the seams with right sides together, 5mm (¼in) from the edges.

Front body Place the two larger front body pieces (A) right sides together and stitch the straight edge, slipping three loops of cord between the two (note which way these will be when the fabric is turned out). Turn out, fold along the seam to enclose the raw edges and press. Sew the two smaller front body pieces (B) together along the straight edge, fold along the seam and press. Sew the buttons on to B opposite the loops. Butt the folded straight edges of the two front pieces together and tack together at the ends.

Head Stitch one head piece to the front body pieces, making sure the two front pieces are tightly butted together. Embroider the eyes, nose and mouth on the head. Stitch the other head piece to the back body at the neck edge.

Ears, legs and arms Stitch the ears, legs and arms together in matched pairs, leaving the straight edge open; turn right side out.

Assembly Place the back and front pieces right sides together. Slip the limbs and ears in position, matching the raw edges so that they will be the right way when the pieces are turned out. Stitch all round, leaving a gap in one side for turning. Turn out and stitch the gap closed.

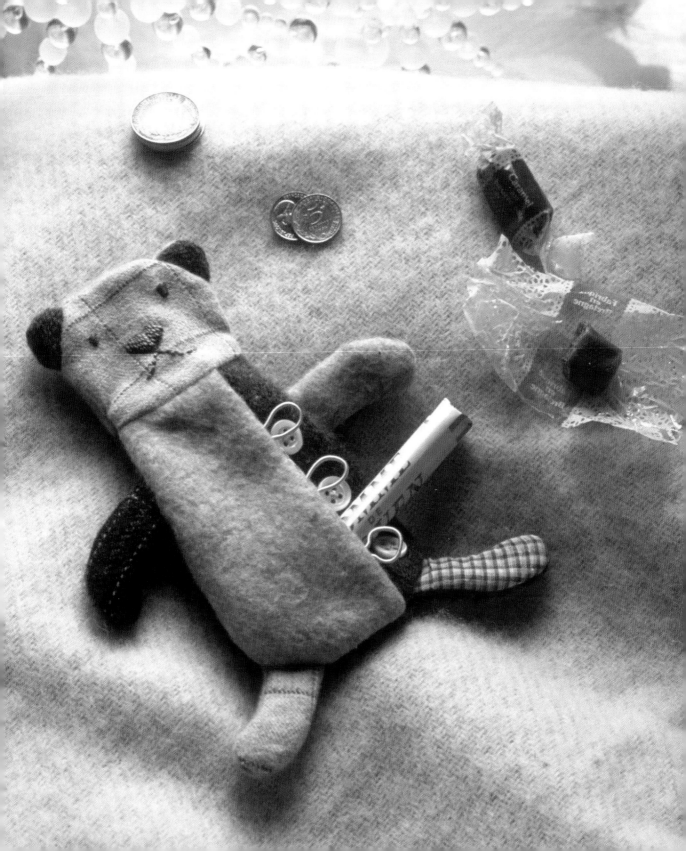

Bright colours and fun designs

Bear wallet *(continued)*

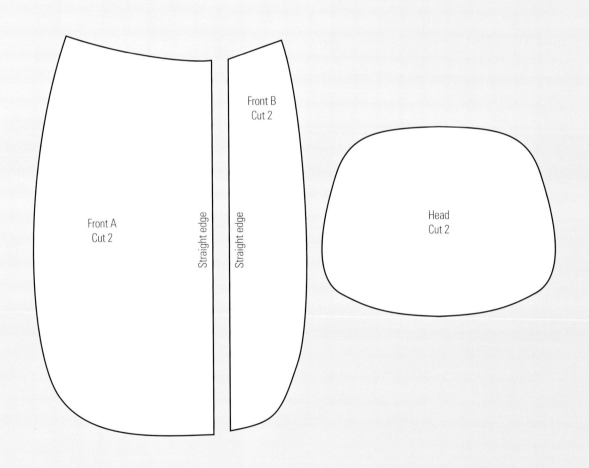

Front A
Cut 2

Front B
Cut 2

Straight edge

Straight edge

Head
Cut 2

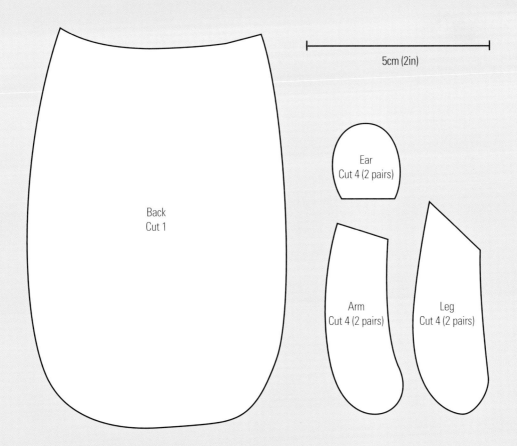

5cm (2in)

Back
Cut 1

Ear
Cut 4 (2 pairs)

Arm
Cut 4 (2 pairs)

Leg
Cut 4 (2 pairs)

Bright colours and fun designs

Big blue dog

Dimensions

Length about 1m (39½in)

Materials

100 × 140cm (39½ × 55in) printed fabric for the main parts of the dog ▪ plain cotton remnant for the nose ▪ checked cotton fabric remnants for the ears, belly and legs ▪ synthetic stuffing ▪ lavender (optional) ▪ sewing thread

Method

Enlarge the patterns on pages 68–69 to size (see page 2) and pin them to the printed fabric. Cut out the following from folded fabric, adding 1cm (⅜in) seam allowances all round: two bodies, four front legs, two outside back legs and two inside back legs. From checked fabric cut four ears, two 5 × 95cm (2 × 37½in) strips (B) for the front legs and two 5 × 115cm (2 × 45¼in) strips (C) for the back legs. You will also need an 8 × 170cm (3 × 67in) strip to run from the nape of the dog's neck, over the face, round and under the belly to the tail (A). Use checked fabric for this or patterned fabric for the head and checked fabric for the belly section.

Ears Stitch the ears together in pairs, right sides facing, leaving the top open; turn out. Pin an ear in position on the head of each body piece.

Body With right sides facing, pin and then stitch strip A to one body piece, varying its width according to the location. The strip begins as a point at the nape of the neck and is at its maximum width on the top and around the head, becoming a little smaller at the level of the front neck. The strip regains its full width on the belly and finishes by fading to a point under the tail (see the pattern, page 69). Attach the other side of the strip to the second body piece in the same way. Stitch the two body pieces right sides together along the back and around the tail, leaving a gap in the centre of the back; turn out. Fill with stuffing and lavender. Close up the gap.

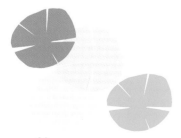

Legs With right sides facing, stitch a strip B between each pair of front-leg pieces, leaving a gap to turn through and joining the ends of the strips neatly. Stitch each strip C between one outside back leg and one inside back leg in the same way, but finishing the strips at the top of the inside leg on each side, so that the top of the back leg is not joined. Turn out and stuff the legs. Sew the front legs securely to the strip of checked fabric and in the hollow of the dog's body. Sew the outside back legs in place and fill the void at the top of the leg with stuffing. Sew the inside leg to the strip under the belly.

Nose Cut out a plain cotton fabric octagon for the nose; make a small hem all round and then attach to the dog with slipstitch.

Tip: This pattern is a bit more complicated than most of the others in this book, so read through all the instructions before you begin to make sure you understand how the dog is constructed.

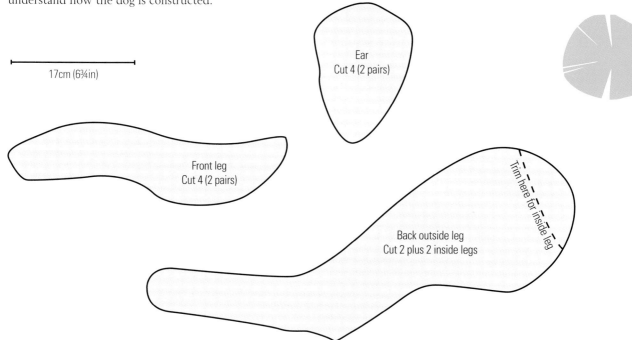

17cm (6¾in)

Ear
Cut 4 (2 pairs)

Front leg
Cut 4 (2 pairs)

Back outside leg
Cut 2 plus 2 inside legs

Trim here for inside leg

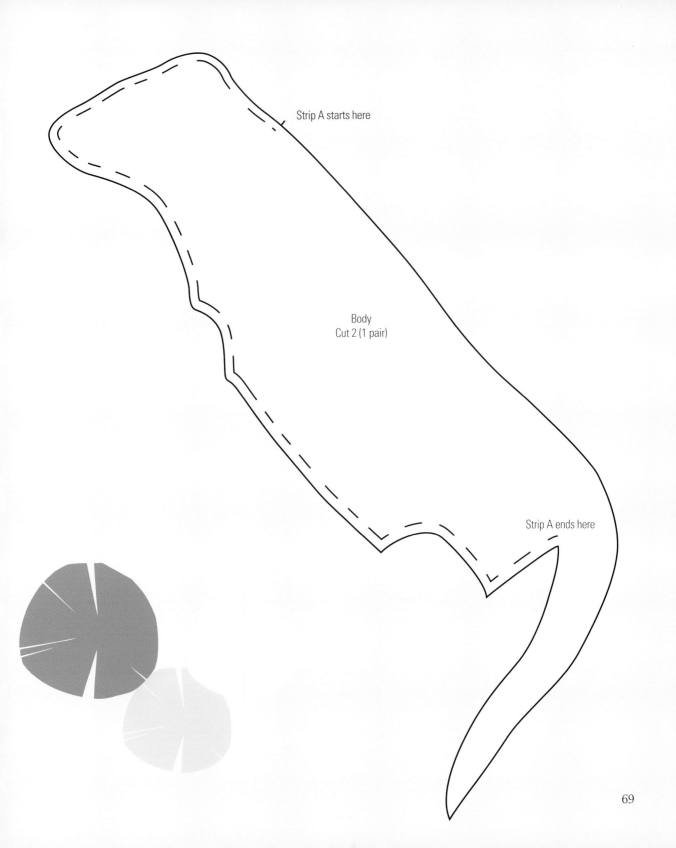

Strip A starts here

Body
Cut 2 (1 pair)

Strip A ends here

Hanging teddy decorations

Materials

For 2 teddies:

Four 10 × 13cm (4 × 5in) rectangles of cotton fabric ● 90cm (1yd) ribbon, 7mm (¼in) wide ● synthetic stuffing

Method

Trace the pattern. Pin the cotton rectangles together in pairs with right sides facing and pin the pattern on top. Cut out, adding 2cm (¾in) seam allowances all round. With right sides facing, stitch each teddy all round, leaving a gap to turn through. Snip into the seam allowances at curves for ease then turn out. Fill with a little stuffing and then close up the gap. Tie a teddy to each end of the ribbon, attaching it around the neck, for hanging.

Tip: The teddy bodies could alternatively be stitched together right sides out using a decorative overcast stitch and the bears could be embellished with ribbons, lace and embroidery in the same way as the rabbits on page 61.

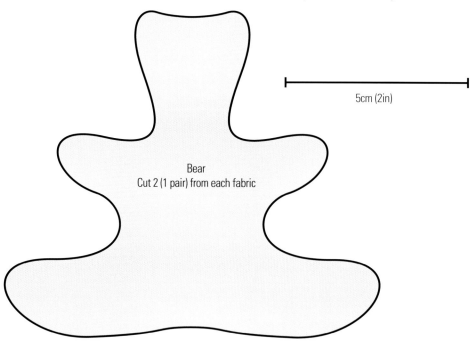

5cm (2in)

Bear
Cut 2 (1 pair) from each fabric

Bright colours and fun designs

Crazy cat and dog

Materials

Assorted fabric remnants ◦ sewing thread, embroidery cotton and wool etc… ◦ wire ◦ synthetic stuffing ◦ fabric glue ◦ buttons

Method

These animals are made from remnants left over from previous projects. Sort the fabrics by colour, texture, size, those which fray and those which do not etc. This will make it easier to pick from the right pile or create new combinations. Do not hesitate to rework the designs to suit your own requirements and style: cut, embroider, decorate with beads and ribbons, pleat and so on.

Limbs Cut one piece of wire for the arms and one for the legs, large enough to extend from one end of the limbs to the other across the body. Cover with fabric glued, knotted and sewn in place, as desired.

Body Cut out two fabric rectangles. Fold a small seam allowance to the wrong side all round then place the two pieces wrong sides together. Slip the arms and legs between the fabric layers and close up the edges, leaving a gap. Stuff the body and then close up the gap.

Head Cut out two pieces as for the body, press seam allowances to the wrong side and then place the two pieces together, right sides out. Add ears made in the same way as the body, catching the ends between the fabric layers before joining. Sew the head to the body.

Clothing Make roughly shaped clothing to fit your dolls depending on what remnants you have available.

Tip: There is no right or wrong way to make these animals. See it as an opportunity to have fun and experiment with the materials you have at your disposal.

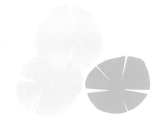

Natural
fabrics

Natural fabrics

Linen teddy

Dimensions

About 45cm (17¾in) tall

Materials

Linen fabric or linen from an old sheet ● Dylon china blue dye ● cotton fabric remnants ● synthetic stuffing ● two brown buttons for eyes ● four small buttons for the jointing ● linen thread ● large needle for thread jointing ● brown embroidery cotton ● ribbon or strip of pink linen for a bow

Method

Dye the linen following the manufacturer's instructions, leave to dry and then iron. Enlarge the patterns on pages 78–79 to size (see page 2). From the cotton fabric remnants cut out the following, adding 7mm (¼in) seam allowances all round: two palms, two soles and one ear. Cut out all the other parts from the linen adding the same seam allowances as before: two outside arms, two inside arms, two fronts, two backs, one centre head, two side heads, four legs and three ears. When joining pieces, stitch the pieces together with right sides facing, taking a 7mm (¼in) seam allowance.

Body Stitch the two front pieces together along the centre-front edge. Stitch the two backs together along the centre back, leaving a gap as indicated on the pattern. Stitch the front to the back all round and turn out through the gap in the back. Stuff the body and close up the gap.

Arms and legs Stitch a palm to each inside arm along the straight edge then stitch each inside arm to an outside arm, leaving a gap as indicated on the pattern. Turn out, stuff and close up the gap. Stitch the legs together in pairs, leaving the straight edge open and a gap in the back of the leg to turn through. Attach the sole to each leg then turn the legs out and stuff them. Close up the gap.

Ears Pair up the ears with right sides facing and stitch all round, leaving the straight edge open. Turn out the ears.

Head Tack then stitch the centre head between the side-head pieces from the nose to the nape of the neck. Stitch the side-head pieces together between the nose and the front neck. Turn out the head and stuff it. Sew the ears in place on the head, tucking in the raw edges at the bottom edge of each one. Embroider the nose and mouth and attach the buttons for eyes. Sew the head to the body.

Attaching the limbs Thread the linen thread through a large needle, stitch at shoulder level to cross the body then pass the needle through an arm. Pass the needle through a button then take the needle back through the button and arm in the other direction to cross the body. Pass the needle through the other arm and another button. Take the needle back through the button and arm and knot securely under the arm to hide the knot. Join the legs to the body in the same way.

Finishing Embroider the claws using linen thread and straight stitches. Tie a ribbon or strip of pink linen around the neck.

Natural fabrics

Linen teddy (continued)

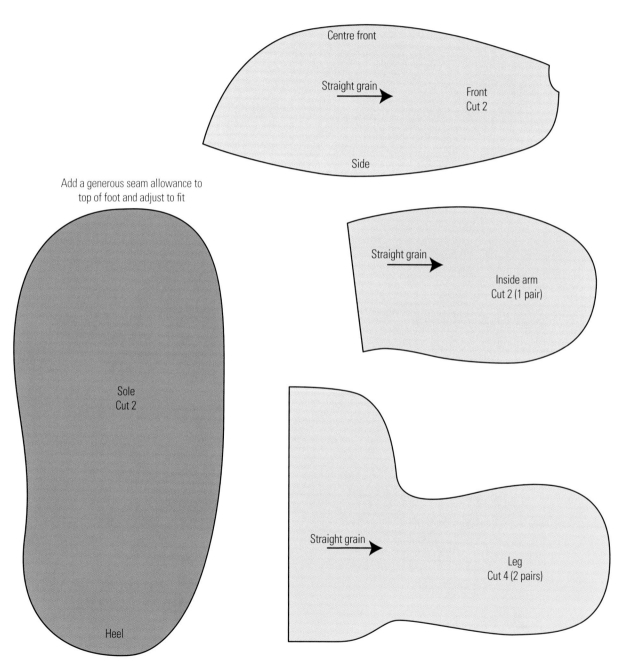

Centre front

Straight grain

Front
Cut 2

Side

Add a generous seam allowance to
top of foot and adjust to fit

Sole
Cut 2

Heel

Straight grain

Inside arm
Cut 2 (1 pair)

Straight grain

Leg
Cut 4 (2 pairs)

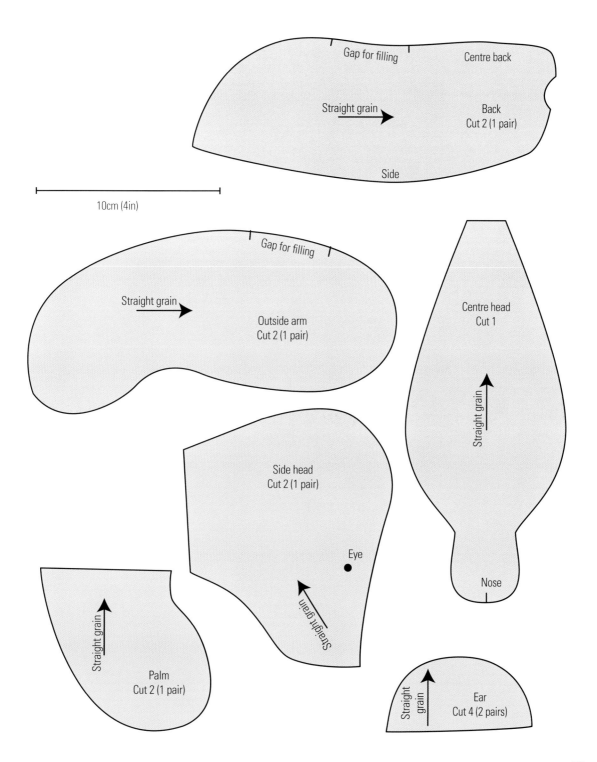

Gap for filling

Centre back

Straight grain

Back
Cut 2 (1 pair)

Side

10cm (4in)

Gap for filling

Straight grain

Outside arm
Cut 2 (1 pair)

Centre head
Cut 1

Straight grain

Side head
Cut 2 (1 pair)

Eye

Straight grain

Straight grain

Nose

Palm
Cut 2 (1 pair)

Straight grain

Ear
Cut 4 (2 pairs)

79

Natural fabrics

Country mouse

Dimensions

25cm (10in) tall

Materials

20 × 50cm (8 × 20in) rectangle of unbleached closely woven fabric for the mouse • 10 × 50cm (4 × 20in) strip of fabric for the shirt • 20 × 30cm (8 × 12in) rectangle of woollen fabric for the trousers • 18 × 3cm (7 × 1¼in) rectangle of woollen fabric for the scarf • synthetic stuffing • ecru thread and thread to match the fabrics • two small buttons • black pearl cotton

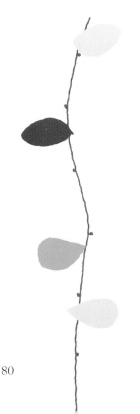

Method

Enlarge the body patterns on page 82 to size – you can redraw them on dressmakers' squared paper or use a photocopier. Cut the pieces from the closely woven fabric the number of times indicated, adding a small seam allowance around each piece. When joining pieces, stitch them together with right sides facing where possible, bearing in mind that sometimes it may be easier to sew them wrong sides together with the seam allowances turned under.

Mouse Stitch the centre head to the two side-head pieces from nose to nape of neck. Stitch the two side-head pieces together from nose to front neck edge. Turn out and stuff the head. Fold each ear right sides together and stitch around the edge, leaving a gap; turn out and close up the gap. Fold the arms and legs in the same way and sew all round, leaving the top edge open. Turn out and stuff each limb. Place the two parts of the body right sides together and position the arms so that they will be caught in the seam and sit correctly when the body is turned out. Stitch the pieces together, leaving the bottom open. Turn out and stuff the body. Turn in the seam allowances at the bottom edge of the body, slip the tops of the legs inside and then close up the seam. Sew the head to the body. Join the two parts of the tail and attach the tail in position on the body. Sew the ears to each side of the head. Embroider the claws, eyes, nose and mouth with black straight stitch. If you wish, add whiskers from short lengths of black pearl cotton (see the photograph).

Trousers or dungarees Cut out two trouser pieces and the two pockets using the diagrams on page 83 and without adding seam allowances. For the dungarees, add the bib at the top of the front. The line BD marks where the inside leg seam begins. Place the two pieces together with right sides facing and edges matching and stitch the centre-back seam from A to B, leaving a gap for the tail. Now stitch the centre front from C to D or E to D. Fold each leg in half with right sides facing and stitch the inside-leg seams from BD to the lower edge. Sew a pocket on to each front, turning the raw edges under and stitching in place with small stitches. For the braces, cut out two 1 × 10cm (⅜ × 4in) strips for the trousers or two 1 × 7cm (⅜ × 2¾in) strips for the dungarees. Oversew the edges if the fabric frays. Stitch the braces to the back then attach to the front with a decorative button.

Country mouse (*continued*)

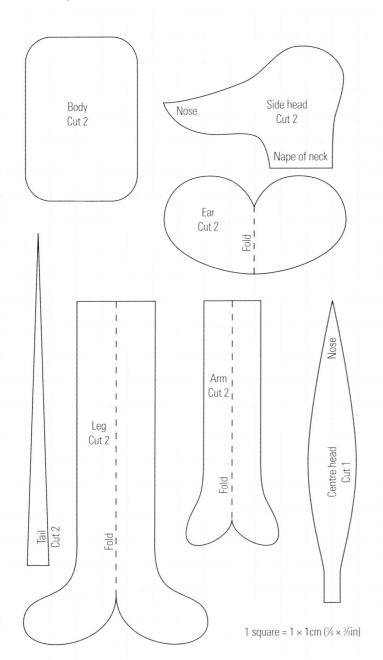

Body
Cut 2

Nose

Side head
Cut 2

Nape of neck

Ear
Cut 2

Fold

Tail
Cut 2

Leg
Cut 2

Fold

Fold

Arm
Cut 2

Fold

Nose

Centre head
Cut 1

1 square = 1 × 1cm (⅜ × ⅜in)

Shirt Sew the fronts to the back at the shoulders. Stitch the sleeves to the armholes. Stitch each sleeve underarm and adjacent side in one go. Matching the centre of the collar to the centre-back of the shirt, pin the collar's right side to the wrong side of the shirt neck. Pin in place around the neck and then stitch in place. Flip the collar over to the right side and press. Turn a small hem all round the raw edge of the collar and stitch in place.

Scarf Fringe the ends of the rectangle of woollen fabric and then tie it around the mouse's neck.

Tip: Stitch the tail pieces together with right sides out because they are too small to join easily the other way. Alternatively, use a piece of cotton cord for the tail.

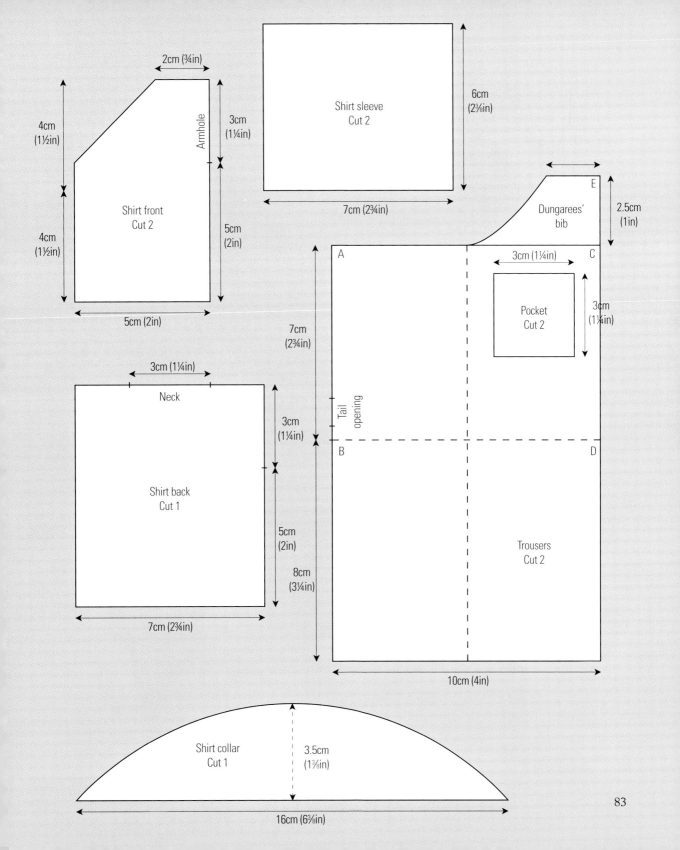

2cm (¾in)

4cm
(1½in)

Armhole

3cm
(1¼in)

Shirt sleeve
Cut 2

6cm
(2⅜in)

Shirt front
Cut 2

5cm
(2in)

7cm (2¾in)

E

Dungarees'
bib

2.5cm
(1in)

4cm
(1½in)

5cm (2in)

A

3cm (1¼in)

C

3cm
(1¼in)

3cm (1¼in)

Neck

3cm
(1¼in)

7cm
(2¾in)

Pocket
Cut 2

Tail opening

Shirt back
Cut 1

3cm
(1¼in)

B

D

5cm
(2in)

Trousers
Cut 2

8cm
(3¼in)

7cm (2¾in)

10cm (4in)

Shirt collar
Cut 1

3.5cm
(1⅜in)

16cm (6⅜in)

83

Patchwork bear

Materials

70cm (¾yd) patchwork-printed cotton fabric, 110cm (43in) wide or cotton fabric remnants ● 500g (1lb) synthetic stuffing ● two buttons for the eyes ● small piece of brown felt for the nose ● ribbon for a bow

Method

Enlarge the parts of the pattern from pages 86–87 to size. Fold the fabric in half, right sides together, and then pin the patterns to the wrong side, thinking of how the patchwork pattern will work on the bear – triangle in the middle of the front, similar legs and arms etc. Respect the straight grains (marked with arrows) so that the bear is not stretched out of shape when you stuff him. Cut out the pieces the number of times indicated – 5mm (¼in) seam allowances are included. Cut the nose section of the centre-front head piece in felt without adding seam allowances. When joining the pieces, use the numbered notches to help with positioning (see the patterns) and stitch all pieces together with right sides facing.

Ears Stitch the ears together in pairs around the outer curved edge. Turn out and fill lightly with stuffing. Tack the open edge of the ears together without turning the seam allowances in.

Head Sew the buttons for eyes in position on the side-front head pieces. Join each side-front head to a side-back head, matching notches 1 and 2 and attaching the ears in the seam. Lay the felt nose in position on the centre-front head piece and topstitch along the edge where it joins the main part of the centre-front piece. Join the centre-front to the centre-back head, matching notch 3, then join the centre heads to the side heads, leaving the opening and making sure the felt nose is stitched in the seam. Stitch the side-front heads together from the tip of the nose to the neck.

Body Join the two fronts together along the centre-front seam, matching notch 6 then join the two backs together from notch 7 to the bottom (pointed end). Join the front to the back, aligning notch 8. Join the shoulders with a few stitches.

Arms and legs Fold each arm in half, aligning notch 9, and stitch the seam (which runs round the paw), leaving the top (10 and 11) open. Turn out the arms and attach to the body. Fold each leg in half and stitch the inside-leg seam, aligning notch 12. Attach the sole to the bottom, aligning notch 13. Turn out the legs and sew to the body.

Finishing With right sides out, join the head to the body then stuff the bear through the opening in the back, distributing the filling evenly. Close up the back with secure stitching by hand. Tie a ribbon around the bear's neck to finish.

Patchwork bear
(continued)

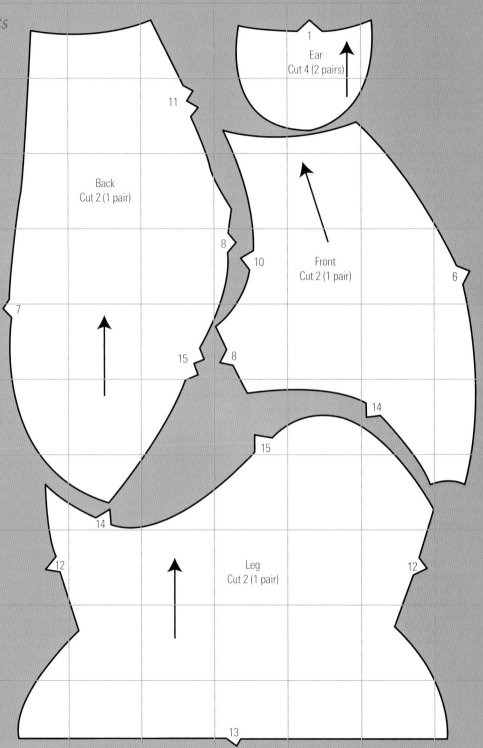

1
Ear
Cut 4 (2 pairs)

11

Back
Cut 2 (1 pair)

8

10

Front
Cut 2 (1 pair)

6

7

15

8

14

15

14

12

Leg
Cut 2 (1 pair)

12

13

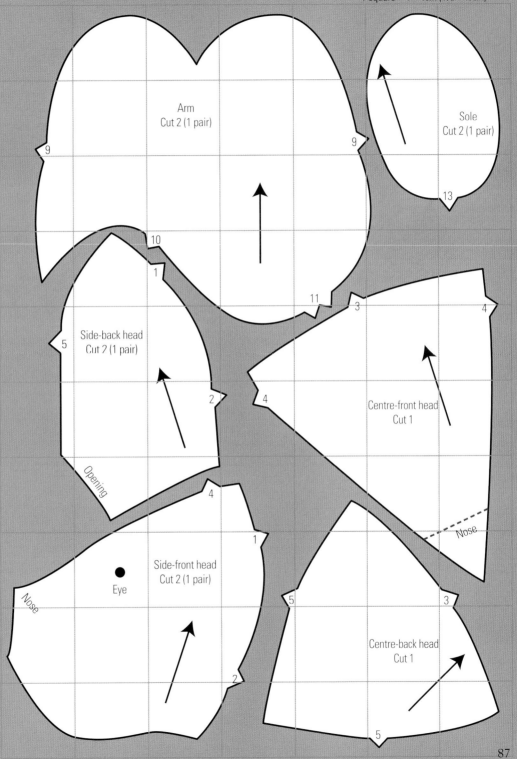

1 square = 4 × 4cm (1½ × 1½in)

Arm
Cut 2 (1 pair)

Sole
Cut 2 (1 pair)

9

9

13

10

1

11

3

4

Side-back head
Cut 2 (1 pair)

5

2

4

Centre-front head
Cut 1

4

Opening

4

1

Nose

Side-front head
Cut 2 (1 pair)

Eye

Nose

5

3

Centre-back head
Cut 1

2

5

87

Patchwork cow

Materials

45 × 30cm (17¾ × 12in) rectangle of plain cotton fabric for the back • printed cotton fabric remnants for the front • synthetic stuffing • 45 × 30cm (17¾ × 12in) synthetic wadding (batting) • card or template plastic • white sewing thread • fine blue yarn • pink ribbon

Method

Patchwork Cut out a 7 × 7cm (2¾ × 2¾in) template from card or template plastic and use it to cut 36 fabric squares from the cotton remnants, repeating fabrics as often as you like. Join the squares into strips of six and then sew the strips together to make a patchwork of 6 × 6 squares, taking a 1cm (⅜in) seam allowance. Pin the patchwork to the wadding (batting) and then work white running stitch through both layers 1cm (⅜in) from each side of every seam.

Cow Enlarge the cow pattern to size. Pin it to the plain cotton fabric and cut out, adding 5mm (¼in) all round for a seam allowance. Repeat to cut out the patchwork, placing the fabric slightly on the bias (see the photograph). Pin the plain cow to the patchwork one with right sides facing and stitch all round, leaving a gap in the back. Turn the cow right sides out, stuff it and then close the gap with small stitches. Plait some fine blue yarn together for the tail and knot the end. Attach this to the back of the cow. Tie the ribbon around the cow's neck and tie in a bow.

Tip: For speedy results, use a printed patchwork fabric for the front of the cow instead of making the patchwork from scratch. You could use the same fabric for the back of the cow too.

1 square = 5 × 5cm (2 × 2in)

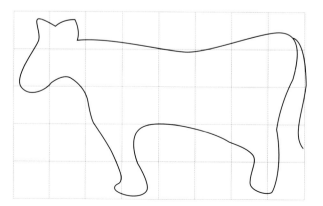

Floor-cloth dog

Materials

Unbleached floor cloth ● red pearl cotton ● black embroidery cotton ● strong sewing thread to match the cloth

Method

Cut out one a 17 × 13cm (6¾ × 5in) rectangle for the body, a 12 × 8cm (4¾ × 3in) rectangle for the head and four 13 × 9cm (5 × 3½in) rectangles for the legs. Cut the ears and tail from the remnants. Fold the body in half and then in half again. Oversew the edges using red pearl cotton to secure them and to prevent fraying. Roll the leg rectangles and then stitch securely in the same way. Stitch the bottom of the legs also. Fold the head rectangle in half three times to make eight layers. Shape to obtain a fairly long head and stitch down. Make the ears in the same way by folding remnants and stitching in red thread. For the tail, use a thin piece of cloth folded and stitched in matching thread. Join all the pieces then embroider the eyes, nose and mouth in black.

Tip: Add your own creative flair with an alternative tail by knitting a red i-cord version or using cotton cord, braid or plaited wool.

Cloth dogs

Dimensions

Make dogs of different sizes simply by enlarging or reducing the patterns on a photocopier.

Materials

For the large dog:
30cm (12in) cotton fabric, 140cm (55in) wide
● brown cotton fabric remnants for the ear(s) and eye patches ● black embroidery cotton ● sewing thread ● woollen fabric remnant and a sock for the clothes ● cord, ribbon or shoelaces to tie the trousers at the waist ● synthetic stuffing

Method

Enlarge the patterns on pages 94–95 to size. Cut out the body pieces the number of times indicated, adding 5mm (¼in) all the way round for the seams. If you wish, cut one or two of the ear pieces from brown fabric. When joining pieces, stitch the seams with right sides facing, 5mm (¼in) from the edges.

Body and arms Join the two front pieces together at the centre-front edge. Join the two back pieces at the centre-back edge. Join the back to the front all round but leaving the neck open. Stuff the body.

Head Close up the darts on the side-head pieces. Sew each side-head piece to the centre-head piece, matching the horizontal line on the centre-head piece with the nose on the side-head pieces. Stitch the ears together in pairs with right sides facing, leaving the base edge open. Turn out the ears and close up the base, tucking the seam allowances in. Stuff the head and then attach it to the body. Attach the ears just behind the darts.

Legs Sew the legs together in pairs with right sides facing, leaving the top and bottom open. Insert the sole of the foot; turn out. Stuff the legs and close up the top. Attach the legs to the bottom of the body.

Tail Fold the tail in half and sew the long seam, leaving the end open. Trim the seam allowance short at the tip. Turn out the tail, stuff it and then stitch it to the bottom of the back.

Face Cut out a piece of brown cotton fabric, turn a small hem all round and stitch it to the head to make a patch. Embroider the eyes, nose, mouth and whiskers. Mark the claws with black straight stitching.

Trousers Cut out two trouser pieces on the fold, adding 2cm (¾in) all round for seams and hems. Fold in half with right sides facing and stitch the inside-

Cloth dogs *(continued)*

leg seams. Slip one leg into the other, right sides facing. Stitch the centre back and front seam in one go. Hem the bottom of the legs and then the waist. Slide a length of cord or ribbon into the hem of the waist to tighten the trousers.

Shirt Cut out the shirt from folded fabric, adding 5mm (¼in) all round for seams. Before unfolding, cut up the fold from the bottom of the front piece to the neck to separate the front into its two parts and then make the cut for the neck. Fold the shirt in half then stitch the sides and sleeve underarms. Hem the sleeves. Open the front and neck and make a tiny rolled hem; stitch it in place. Hem both ends and one long edge of the collar. Attach the collar to the neck, matching the raw edges. Sew a decorative button under the collar.

Shoes Cut out the pattern twice on the fold, adding 5mm (¼in) all round for seams. Fold each shoe in half and sew the front from A to B. Attach the sole. Slide a shoe on to each foot. Use a short length of thread for the laces.

Vest Cut this from a sock, making one hole for the head and two holes for the arms. Sew small hems around the raw edges.

Tip: Each of the dogs in the photograph on page 93 is wearing different clothing. You can have lots of fun making additional dogs and dressing them differently too. If you like to knit, why not knit them waistcoats and jumpers? If you enjoy patchwork, you could make a girl dog with a patchwork dress and a bag. If dressmaking is your hobby, you could stitch them some tailored clothes and so on.

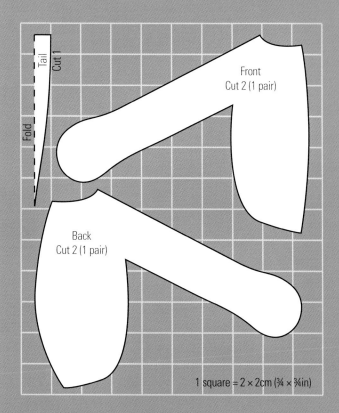

Tail Cut 1

Fold

Front
Cut 2 (1 pair)

Back
Cut 2 (1 pair)

1 square = 2 × 2cm (¾ × ¾in)

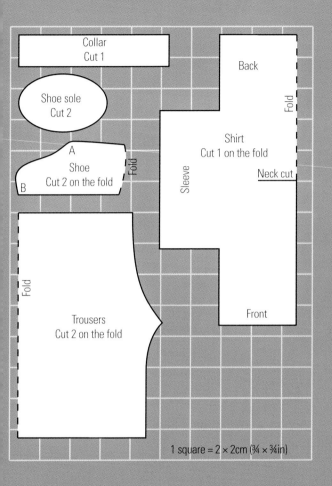

Collar
Cut 1

Shoe sole
Cut 2

A
Shoe
Cut 2 on the fold
B

Fold

Back

Fold

Shirt
Cut 1 on the fold

Sleeve

Neck cut

Front

Fold

Trousers
Cut 2 on the fold

1 square = 2 × 2cm (¾ × ¾in)

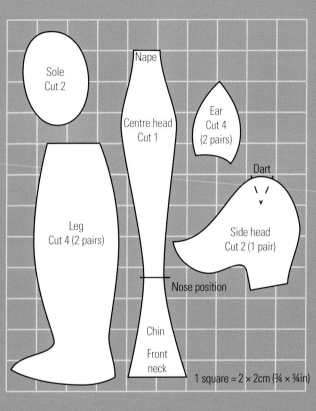

Sole
Cut 2

Nape

Centre head
Cut 1

Ear
Cut 4
(2 pairs)

Dart

Leg
Cut 4 (2 pairs)

Nose position

Side head
Cut 2 (1 pair)

Chin

Front
neck

1 square = 2 × 2cm (¾ × ¾in)

Natural fabrics

Hobbyhorse

Materials

1.50m (60in) natural linen ● white thread ● remnants of green fabric ● synthetic stuffing ● brown linen thread ● reel of string or cord ● brown embroidery cotton ● two 2.5cm (1in) diameter buttons for eyes ● two 8mm (⅜in) diameter buttons for the nostrils ● broom handle, approximately 1.10m (43in) long ● erasable fabric pen

Method

Head Draw all the pieces on the wrong side of the linen. Cut out, adding 1cm (⅜in) all round for seam allowances. Stitch the ears together in pairs with right sides facing, leaving the curved base edge open. Turn out and then slip a little stuffing into each one. Tack an ear to each side head in the position marked on the pattern. Stitch all the remaining pieces together with right sides facing, 1cm (⅜in) from the edges, ensuring that the lettered edges match. Leave the back open. Turn out and stuff before closing up the head but leaving the opening at the bottom end for the broom handle.

Decorations Cut out two triangles and two squares from green fabric and attach to the inside of the ears and the cheeks using large stitching and linen thread. Sew on the small buttons for the nostrils and the large ones for the eyes, using the brown embroidery cotton. Embroider the mouth with large cross stitches. Braid the cord to obtain a piece approximately 1m (40in) long. Sew to each end of the mouth for a rein. Untwist more of the string or cord to separate the strands and cut into long pieces. Use backstitch to attach bundles of the strands tightly to the back of the head for the mane. Slide the broom handle into the head and secure it with several turns of very tight cord around the fabric. Tie securely.

Tip: You do not have to use a broom handle for this hobbyhorse. If you look closely at the one in the photograph, you will see that it is actually a stick of bamboo.

Little ghosts

Materials

White fabric remnant ● synthetic stuffing ● small mother-of-pearl buttons ● very fine cotton cord for hair (optional) ● fine string or twine ● white sewing thread ● DMC stranded embroidery cotton in ivory (optional) ● extra-strong glue (optional) ● dressmakers' carbon paper

Method

Ghost Enlarge the patterns to size (see page 2). Fold the fabric in half with right sides facing and use the carbon paper to copy the pattern for your chosen ghost on top. If you want to add hair, cut 3cm (1¼in) lengths of cotton cord and separate the strands as far as possible. Lay them in position on top of your ghost so that they will be caught in the seam (noting which end of the string will be on the outside when the ghost is turned out). Keeping the layers together, stitch along the ghostly outline all round, leaving a gap of 3–4cm (1¼ – 1½in) at the bottom. Cut out 3mm (⅛in) outside the seam and then turn out your ghost very carefully, pushing the shapes out. Stuff the ghost and then close up the gap by hand with small, invisible stitches.

Embellishments Glue or stitch on the buttons for the eyes and then decorate your little phantom, embroidering a small heart, attaching a fabric patch or making a fake repair with the embroidery cotton etc. Thread a piece of string through the top of the head to hang up the ghost.

Tip: When making these for children, you could add a few choice swirls of glow-in-the-dark dimensional paint or stitch on some glow-in-the-dark buttons.

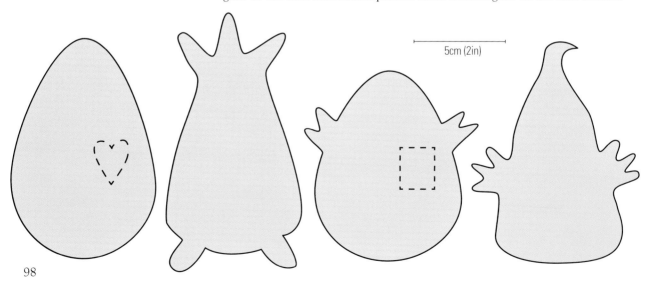

5cm (2in)

Cat dolls

Dimensions

Daddy: 34cm (13½in)
Mummy: 32cm (12½in)
Youngster: 28cm (11in)

Materials

Old woollen fabric for the bodies • 25cm (10in) of velvet in each of pearl grey, aubergine, maroon, brown and petrol blue • matching sewing threads • synthetic stuffing • a few buttons • mohair yarn and 4mm (UK 8, US 6) knitting needles for the scarf • fine yarn or embroidery cotton plus an appropriate needle for facial features and whiskers

Method

Enlarge the patterns on pages 102–103 to size (see page 2).

Cats Fold the selected fabrics with right sides facing and place your chosen cat's body pattern on top, placing the centre on the fold. Cut out, adding 5mm (¼in) all round for seam allowances. Embroider the eyes, nose and mouth on one of the body pieces, fastening off the threads securely so that they cannot be pulled out. Pin the body pieces together with right sides facing and stitch all round 5mm (¼in) from the edges, leaving a 5cm (2in) gap under one arm. Notch the seam allowances for ease. Turn out and stuff, retaining some flexibility. Close up the gap.

Whiskers Cut strands of fine yarn or embroidery cotton and, using a long needle, thread them through both sides of the head and fasten with a knot level with the fabric.

Cutting out the clothes Fold the velvet with right sides facing and pin the patterns on top, placing the centres on the fold as indicated. Seam allowances are not required because the seams are oversewn; cut round the patterns the number of times indicated.

Shirt/top Pin the two shirt pieces right sides together and then oversew the top arm/shoulder seams, underarm and side seams. Hem the raw edges. To add a small pocket to the daddy's shirt, cut out a small rectangle from a remnant and stitch it on.

Skirt Stitch the back and front pieces together at the sides with right sides facing. Hem the waist and bottom edges.

Trousers Place the trouser pieces together in pairs with right sides facing and oversew the inside-leg and outside-leg seams. Slide one leg into the other, right sides facing and stitch the seam from waist edge to waist edge in one go. Turn out and then hem the legs and waist. For the braces, cut out two 3 × 25cm (1¼ × 10in) strips. Fold a small hem along each long edge then fold lengthways, with wrong sides together, matching the folded edges. Stitch the folded edges together. Fix the braces to the trousers with buttons sewn through all layers.

Scarf Cast on 6 stitches, knit 30cm (12in) in garter stitch (knit every row) and then cast off.

Cat dolls *(continued)*

5cm (2in)

Daddy
Cut 2

Place on fold

Mummy
Cut 2

Place on fold

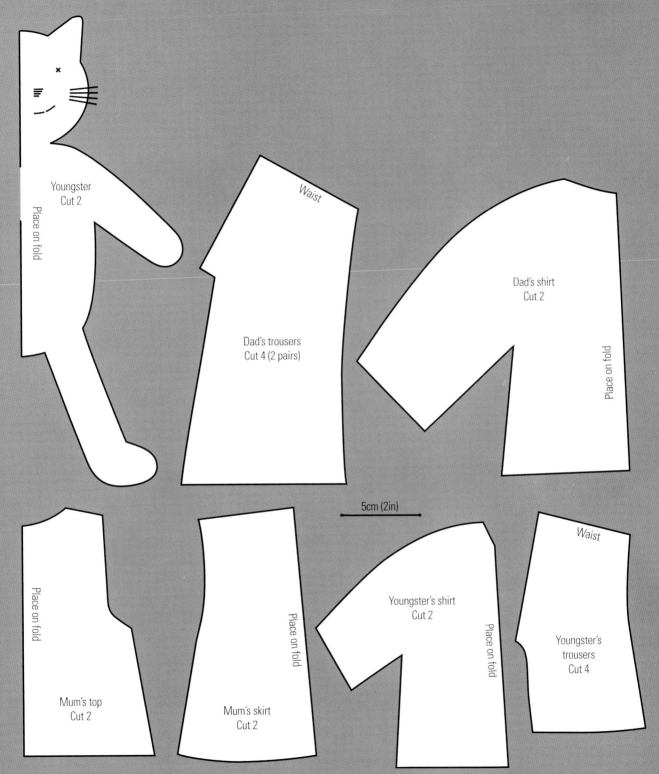

Youngster
Cut 2

Place on fold

Waist

Dad's trousers
Cut 4 (2 pairs)

Dad's shirt
Cut 2

Place on fold

5cm (2in)

Place on fold

Mum's top
Cut 2

Place on fold

Mum's skirt
Cut 2

Youngster's shirt
Cut 2

Place on fold

Waist

Youngster's
trousers
Cut 4

White mouse

Dimensions

18cm (7in) long

Materials

20 × 25cm (8 × 10in) white cotton fabric (old sheet for example) ● white and brown thread ● stiff brown thread such as linen thread ● synthetic stuffing ● 15cm (6in) of white cord for the tail

Method

Enlarge the patterns to size. Cut out two body pieces and four ears – 4mm (⅛in) seam allowances are included. Stitch the two bodies right sides together, leaving a gap in the bottom as indicated on the pattern. Stitch the ears together in pairs, in the same way, leaving the straight bottom edge open. Turn out the body and ears. Stuff the body and close up the gap. Fold the raw edges of the ears to the inside and then stitch closed. Make a little vertical fold before sewing the ears in place. Embroider the eyes and nose using straight stitch and the brown thread. Cut lengths of stiff thread for the whiskers. Thread them on both sides of the muzzle. Tie each side flush with the fabric to fasten. Sew the cord to the back of the body for the tail.

Tip: Make a whole family of mice, creating smaller versions by not enlarging the pattern or even reducing it. Make the mice in different colours too, using up remnants from other projects.

Ears
Cut 4

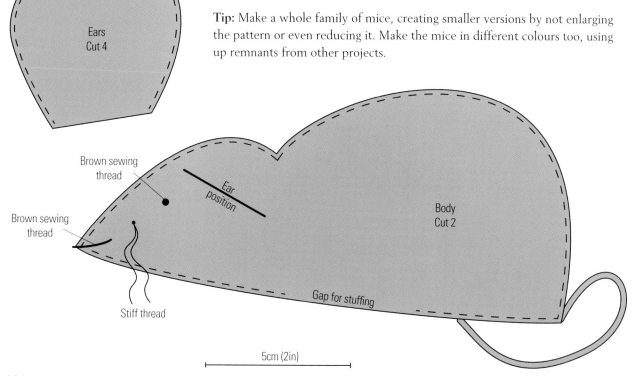

Brown sewing thread

Brown sewing thread

Stiff thread

Ear position

Body
Cut 2

Gap for stuffing

5cm (2in)

Fox stole

Materials

30cm (12in) fake fur, 140cm (55in) wide
• 30cm (12in) natural linen, 140cm (55in)
wide • two mother-of-pearl buttons, 1.5cm
(⅝in) in diameter, for eyes • wadding
(batting) • sewing thread

Method

Wash and iron the linen to preshrink it. Enlarge the patterns for the head and
ears from pages 108–109 (see page 2) and cut out to obtain templates. Cut
two head and two ear pieces from linen then cut the ears twice more from
fake fur. Draw up the remaining two patterns to size and cut them both twice
from fur fabric. The body is 60 × 20cm (24 × 8in) with rounded ends and the
tail is 40 × 20cm (16 × 8in).

Head Stitch each fur ear to a linen one with right sides facing, leaving the
straight base edge open; turn out. Sew the button eyes to one head. Position the
ears on the head piece with the eyes, matching the raw edges and positioning
the ears at the marks on the head piece. Stitch the two heads together with
right sides facing, leaving the top seam open; turn.

Body and tail Stitch the two body pieces together with right sides facing,
leaving gaps at each end where the pattern is shaded. Turn out the body and
tuck in the seam allowances at the gaps but do not stitch yet. Stitch the two tail
pieces together with right sides facing, leaving the straight edge open; turn out.

Assembly Stuff the head with a little wadding. Tuck the open end into one
end of the body and hand stitch in place. Tuck the tail into the other end of
the body and stitch in place in the same way.

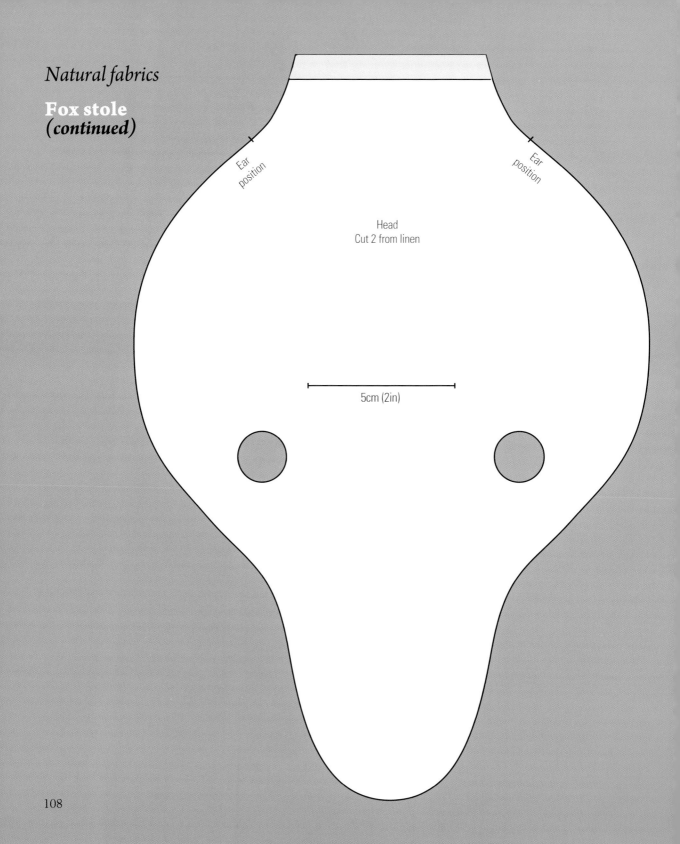

Natural fabrics

Fox stole
(continued)

Ear
position

Ear
position

Head
Cut 2 from linen

5cm (2in)

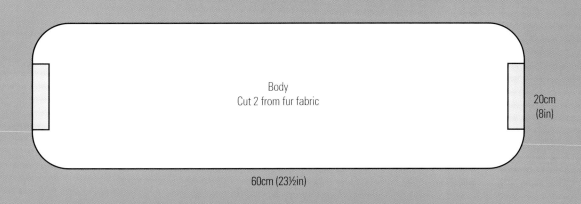

Body
Cut 2 from fur fabric

20cm
(8in)

60cm (23½in)

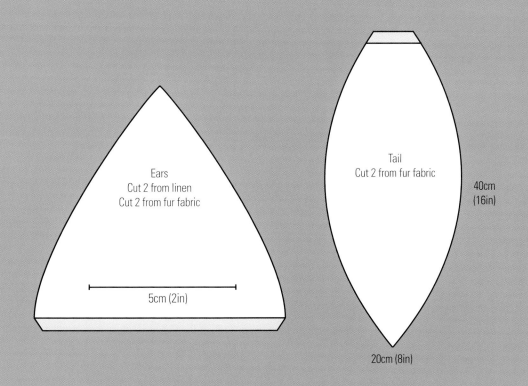

Ears
Cut 2 from linen
Cut 2 from fur fabric

5cm (2in)

Tail
Cut 2 from fur fabric

40cm
(16in)

20cm (8in)

Appliqué

Introduction to appliqué

What is appliqué?

'Appliqué' is a means of decorating a fabric by sewing on one or more fabric shapes. On the following pages, you will find a selection of shapes and decorative motifs that will enhance or transform the creations of your choice.

Many of the projects provide opportunities for using up fabric remnants, although you can always buy new fabrics specifically for them. Appliqué usually works best when the fabrics chosen for the appliqué shapes are similar in type to the base fabric – cotton on cotton, for example. Lightweight fabrics are always easier to handle and sew. Felt, which does not fray and can be positioned in any direction, is often chosen for soft models.

Appliqué motifs can be attached with machine satin stitch or with various hand stitches and they can be decorated further with braid or ribbon for an original result.

Appliqué

Butterfly cushion

Dimensions

40 × 60cm (16 × 24in)

Materials

Linen fabric or old sheet ● sewing thread ● a beautiful butterfly image ● assortment of beads, buttons and sewing thread to match the butterfly ● transfer paper ● two press studs ● 40 × 60cm (16 × 24in) cushion pad

Method

Cutting out From the linen cut a top rectangle 42 × 62cm (16½ × 24½in) and one rectangle for the back 42 × 22cm (16½ × 8¾in) and another 42 × 47cm (16½ × 18½in).

Butterfly Scan a beautiful image of a butterfly after enlarging it with a photocopier if necessary. Following the manufacturer's instructions, print the image on to the transfer paper and then place it face down in the centre of the top rectangle. Transfer the image (usually with the use of an iron). Enhance the butterfly by adding beads, buttons and embroidery.

Assembly Stitch a double 1cm (⅜in) hem on one 42cm (16½in) edge of each back piece. Lay out the top piece, right side up, and lay over the back pieces, right side down, with raw edges matching and the hemmed edges overlapping. Stitch all round and then turn out through the gap where the back pieces overlap. Iron, protecting the butterfly. Sew on the two press studs to close up the cover over the cushion pad.

Tip: Butterfly images can be obtained from books, magazines or via the Internet. You can even create your own by tracing a photograph and painting it before scanning.

Appliqué

Birdcage door hanging

Materials

White cotton fabric ● printed cotton fabric ● fabric for backing ● wadding (batting) ● fusible webbing such as Bondaweb ● felt ● bird image ● transfer paper ● fabric adhesive ● 1m (1yd) ribbon for hanging ● ribbons and braid for decoration ● 60cm (¾yd) bias binding ● velvet flowers and leaves

Cage base
Cut 1 in felt

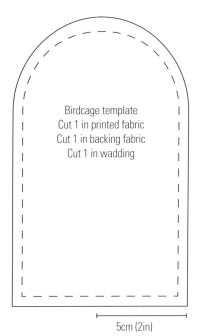

Birdcage template
Cut 1 in printed fabric
Cut 1 in backing fabric
Cut 1 in wadding

5cm (2in)

Method

Enlarge the patterns below using a photocopier and cut out one base in felt and one birdcage in printed cotton, wadding and backing fabric.

Bird Print a bird on to the transfer paper and apply it to white cotton fabric using an iron and following the manufacturer's instructions. Apply fusible webbing to the back and cut out, leaving a border all round, if desired. Fuse the bird in place on the centre of the printed-cotton birdcage.

Birdcage Sew the felt cage base to the printed-cotton birdcage with right sides facing and then turn it down (see the first diagram). Appliqué decorative braids and/or ribbons above the felt, allowing them to overhang by 5mm (¼in) at each end.

Assembly Lay out the backing-fabric birdcage right side down, lay the wadding cage on top and then the printed-cotton cage right side up on top of that. Fold the ribbon for the hanging in half and place the fold at the top of the cage as shown in the second diagram. Tack the bias binding all the way round, along the seamline, covering the ribbon. Sew the layers around the curved edge. Trim the ribbons and the seam allowances where necessary, then turn the binding over to the back and hand stitch it in place. Close up the bottom of the cage and then attach the flowers and leaves.

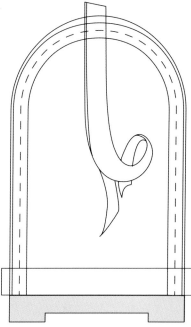

Owl pouch

Dimensions

13 × 10cm (5 × 4in)

Materials

34 × 12cm (13½ × 4¾in) of both blue woollen fabric and printed cotton fabric ● 8 × 10cm (3¼ × 4in) rectangle of beige woollen fabric and remnants of felt in black and white for the owl ● fusible webbing such as Bondaweb ● fabric marker pen ● press stud ● matching sewing thread ● 125cm (1½yd) of braid, 1.5cm (⅝in) wide for the strap ● 125cm (1½yd) of ribbon, 1cm (⅜in) wide for the strap ● pale blue and mid-blue embroidery cottons

Method

Owl Trace the owl pattern (below) and transfer it on to the fusible webbing. Apply the fusible webbing to the back of the beige wool and the black and white felts, following the manufacturer's instructions and using a pressing cloth to avoid overheating the felt. Cut out the owl, face and eye shapes without adding seam allowances. Using the pattern as your guide, fuse the owl to the blue wool rectangle and then fuse on the face and eyes. Secure the felt more firmly by oversewing using matching thread. Work running stitch in the blue embroidery cottons to outline the owl and define its wings.

Pouch Pin the woollen and printed cotton rectangles together with right sides facing. (Seam allowances of 1cm (⅜in) are included.) Draw the curved shape of the flap at one end of the rectangle and trim off the excess fabric 1cm (⅜in) outside the line. Stitch all round 1cm (⅜in) from the edges, leaving the straight end open. Trim or snip into the seam allowances at the curved end and turn out. Fold in the seam allowances at the gap and stitch closed. Make the pouch by folding the rectangle 13cm (5in) from the straight end and close up the sides with small stitches.

Strap Sew the ribbon down the centre of the braid. Turn under the ends of the braid and then stitch it to each side of the pouch, the excess forming a strap. Attach the press stud to form a closure.

Base fold

10cm (4in)

Flap fold

2cm (¾in)

Appliqué

Seagull quilt and pillows

Dimensions

Quilt: 110 × 150cm (43¼ × 59in);
pillows: 33 × 46cm (13 × 18in)

Materials

Cotton fabrics, 140cm (55in) wide: 2.20m
(2½yd) white, 1.52m (1¾yd) each of four
different blues ● DMC pearl cotton No. 5,
in light baby blue 3325 ● sewing thread
● wadding (batting) to fit the quilt ● stuffing
or loose batting

Method

Quilt top For the quilt top, cut out a 29.5 × 152cm (11⅝ × 60in) strip from each of the four blue fabrics. Sew the strips together with right sides facing, taking a 1cm (⅜in) seam allowance. Oversew the raw edges if needed then press open the seams. Enlarge the silhouette of the seagull (see page 122) and then cut it from the white fabric. Oversew the edges then stitch the seagull to the quilt top.

Assembly For the back, cut out a white cotton rectangle measuring 112 × 152cm (44 × 60in). Sew to the quilt top with right sides facing, taking a 1cm (⅜in) seam allowance and leaving a gap to turn through. Turn out, press and then slip the wadding (batting) inside. Close up the gap. Mark the contours of the seagull, its wing and eye with running stitch in pearl cotton, working through all the layers.

Pillow For each pillow, cut out three strips of blue fabric measuring 18 × 35cm (7 × 13¾in) for the top (or play with the widths). Join the strips in the same way as for the quilt. Tack to one layer of wadding (batting). Trace one of the birds on pages 122–123 (enlarged to size), cut it from white fabric and attach it to the front in the same way as for the quilt. For the back, cut out a 35 × 48cm (13¾ × 19in) rectangle of white cotton fabric. Stitch the back to the front with right sides facing, taking a 1cm (⅜in) seam allowance and leaving a gap. Trim off the excess fabric, turn out and fill with stuffing. Close up the gap.

Seagull quilt and pillows *(continued)*

28cm (11in) for the pillow
96cm (37¾in) for the quilt

25cm (9¾in) for the pillow
41cm (16¼in) for the quilt

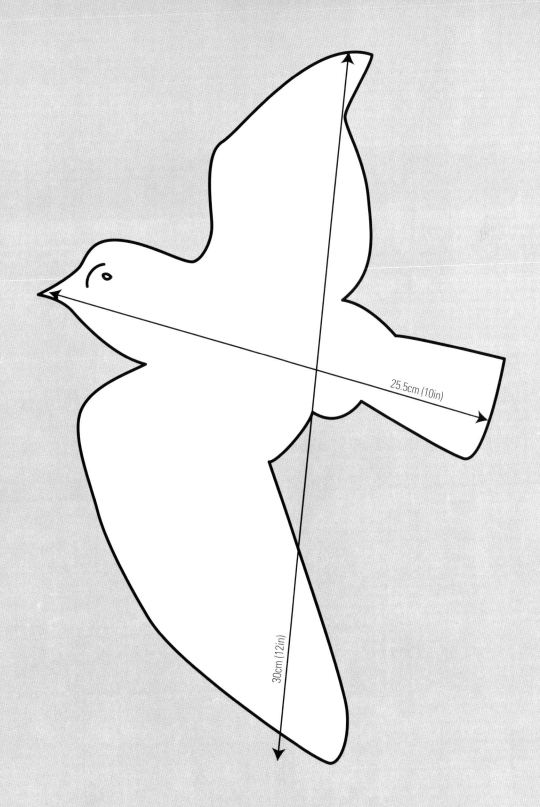

25.5cm (10in)

30cm (12in)

Lucky goldfish glasses pouch

Dimensions

8 × 17cm (3 × 6¾in)

Materials

Two 10 × 22cm (4 × 8¾in) rectangles of unbleached linen fabric ● two 10 × 16cm (4 × 6¼in) rectangles of woven unbleached fabric for lining ● 12 × 6cm (4¾ × 2⅜in) rectangle of orange taffeta for the fish ● white sewing thread ● transfer pencil ● tracing paper ● DMC Stranded Cotton Art 117 in 740, 5282, 645, 647, 740, 99 and 92 ● embroidery needle ● small gold safety pin

Stitches used

Satin stitch, backstitch, straight stitch and chain stitch, worked using two strands of embroidery cotton

Method

Iron a 1cm (⅜in) turning all around each piece of fabric to mark the seamlines; unfold. Enlarge the pattern to size (see page 2) and trace it. Redraw on the wrong side of the tracing paper with the transfer pencil then iron with a very hot iron over one of the linen pieces. Trace the shape of the fish on the taffeta and cut out, adding a small turning allowance all round. Pin the fish in place on the linen and attach with small stitches, folding under the excess as you sew. Embroider the design, following the stitching and colour instructions on the pattern. Press gently with an iron on the wrong side, using a pressing cloth to protect the fabric.

Assembly Pin each linen piece to a lining piece with right sides facing and three edges matching (the linen will be longer) and stitch the matching short edge at the top of the fish. Unfold and press the seam open. Pin the two pieces together with right sides facing, matching the linen to the linen and the lining to the lining. Stitch all round, leaving a 6cm (2⅜in) gap in one edge of the lining to turn through. Turn the fabrics out and close up the gap by hand. Slip the lining inside the case. Attach the gold safety pin.

Thread:
DMC Stranded Cotton Art. 117
A = 740+5282
B = 645
C = 647
D = 740
E = 99
F = 92

Stitches:
1 = satin stitch
2 = backstitch
3 = straight stitch
4 = chain stitch

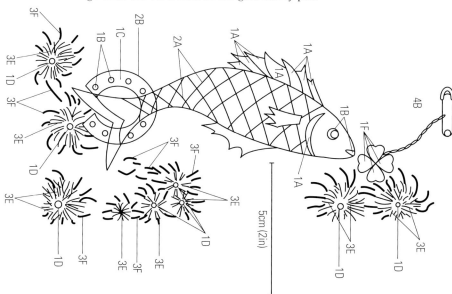

124

Owl scarf

Dimensions

38 × 100cm (15 × 40in)

Materials

120 × 40cm (47¼ × 15¾in) rectangle in each of two cotton fabrics ● 10cm (4in) square of woollen fabric or felt for the body ● remnants of white and black felt ● fusible webbing such as Bondaweb ● matching sewing thread ● embroidery cotton to match the fabric of the scarf

Method

Enlarge the scarf pattern below. Fold each cotton fabric in half with right sides facing then cut the pattern once from each piece, placing the centre on the fabric fold and adding 1cm (⅜in) all round (except at the fold) for the seam allowances.
Owl Trace the body of the owl, face and eyes and transfer to the fusible webbing. Apply to the wool and felt. Cut out on the line. Fuse the eyes to the face and the face to the body and then oversew the pieces in matching thread for extra security. Pin the owl to the point of one of the large rectangles. Fuse in place and then secure with running stitch using the embroidery cotton.
Scarf Pin the two large rectangles together with right sides facing and stitch all round, leaving a gap in the top. Turn out the scarf and close up the gap by hand. Press the edges.

Tip: This owl is also used to decorate the pouch on page 118. Why not make both as a set?

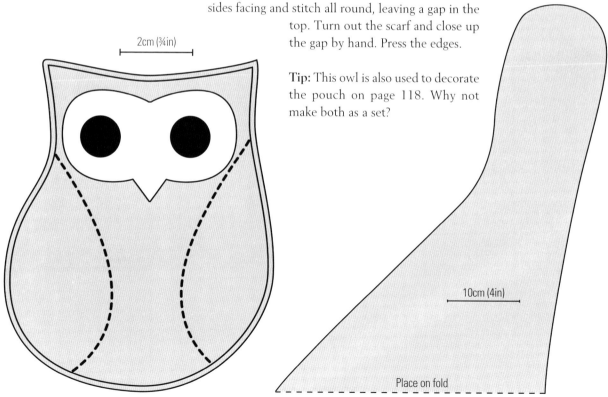

2cm (¾in)

10cm (4in)

Place on fold

Appliqué

Fish notebook

Materials

Notebook with a hard cover ● white cotton fabric (old sheet for example) to make the book cover ● plain and printed fabric remnants ● 60cm (¾yd) fine red ribbon for the tie ● 25cm (10in) red cord for the fish bookmark ● white sewing thread ● red embroidery cotton ● small handful of stuffing or cotton wool

Method

Cover Measure the notebook and then add 3cm (1¼in) to the height and 12cm (4¾in) to the length for the flaps. Cut your white fabric to these measurements. Cut the white fabric in half lengthways and stitch a strip of printed fabric between the halves with right sides facing, to form the spine of the book. Turn 5mm (¼in) then 1cm (⅜in) to the wrong side at the top and bottom and stitch in place.

Large fish Draw a large fish that will fit the front of your notebook on paper and cut out to make a template. Cut from folded fabric to make a matched pair, adding seam allowances all round. Stitch the two parts of the fish together with right sides facing, leaving a small gap on the side to turn through. Notch the seam allowances for ease, turn out and close up the gap. Pin the fish centrally on the front of the book cover. Secure the edges using running stitch and two strands of red embroidery cotton, leaving a gap at the mouth to slide in a pencil.

Fish bookmark Draw two small fish on paper and use each one to cut a pair of fabric fish, adding seam allowances as before. Pin the two parts of each fish together with right sides facing and slip one end of the cord into the mouth of each fish – in order that the cord comes out of the fish's mouth when turned out, lay the cord over the back of the fish and then place the end at the mouth. Stitch the edges, leaving a gap to turn through (where the cord is threaded temporarily) and turn out. Stuff one of the fish and close up the gaps in both fish. Fold the cord in half and stitch to the inside of the cover at the top of the spine, leaving the fishes to hang over the outside.

Assembly Turn 5mm (¼in) then 1cm (⅜in) to the wrong side at each end and stitch in place. Fold over the flaps, using the notebook as your guide, and stitch the flaps down at the top and bottom edges. Cut the fine ribbon in half and stitch a piece to the edge of each flap to close the book by tying.

Corners Cut out two triangles of cotton fabric for the corners, adding 5mm (¼in) for seam allowances all round. Pin in place and attach by hand using invisible stitching.

Fish T-shirt

Materials

Tank top or T-shirt ● three coordinating cotton fabric remnants ● sewing thread to match the top ● embroidery cotton to match the cotton remnants

Method

From each cotton fabric cut out the silhouette of a fish, making sure that the three fish will fit nicely on the top. Pin to the back of the top and then attach with hand or machine stitches, tucking under a small seam allowance as you sew and making sure that you do not stitch through to the front of the garment at the same time by accident. Embroider fishing lines by working running stitches from each fish's mouth towards the shoulder, as if the fish were hanging from a rod.

Tip: It is a bit fiddly turning seam allowances under on curved shapes such as these fish. As an alternative, draw the fish on to fusible webbing, such as Bondaweb, fuse on to the cotton remnants, cut out and then fuse the fish to the back of the top. Secure the edges with a decorative machine or hand stitches.

Appliqué

Fish pillowcases

Materials

White pillowcases ● red and blue floral fabric ● fusible webbing such as Bondaweb ● red and blue embroidery cotton ● mother-of-pearl buttons ● stencils of words and numbers or letters ● stencil brush ● red textile paint

Method

Slip some card into the pillowcases in order to stretch them and prevent the paint from seeping through to the back. Position the stencils to make the words, centring them and keeping to the straight grain – these pillows say 'Le 1er Avril on s'aime' (Everyone loves the 1st April) and 'Poissons d'abord' (Fish first), but you can have whatever words you like, even a child's name. Paint the letters one by one, loading the brush sparingly to prevent drips and to produce a smooth effect. It is better to apply several coats, speeding up the drying with a hairdryer in between coats if necessary.

Draw or trace fish and hearts on to the fusible webbing and cut out, leaving a generous margin all round. Place on the wrong side of the fabrics and iron to fuse. Cut out on the lines then remove the paper backing and fuse the motifs to the pillowcases. Emphasize the edges of the designs with large running stitches in contrasting colours. Sew on the buttons to simulate bubbles and to add the dots over the letter 'I's.

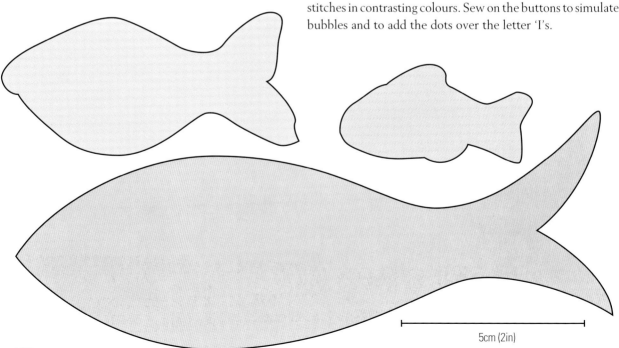

5cm (2in)

Giraffe curtain

Materials

Plain curtain ● fake giraffe fur ● fusible webbing such as Bondaweb ● brown sewing thread ● buttons for the eyes ● embroidery cotton in brown and three shades of green

Method

Trace giraffe silhouettes from books, keeping the outlines simple, and enlarge them to the required size. Trace them on to fusible webbing. Cut out, leaving a margin all round. Fuse the webbing giraffes on to the wrong side of the fake fur then trim exactly round the design. Remove the paper backing and then iron into place on the curtain. Secure the edges of the fabric giraffes with small stitches. Attach buttons for the eyes. Embroider the tails using a single strand of embroidery cotton and create a little tassel at the end. Embroider a few blades of green grass and top some with crossed straight stitches to represent seed heads or flowers.

Winter
warmers

Winter warmers

Lacy cat cushion

Two 53 × 39cm (21 × 15½in) rectangles of black cotton fabric ● 40 × 25cm (15¾ × 10in) each of white silk and black lace ● piece of black-and-white striped ribbon for the collar ● large button ● 150cm (1½yd) narrow black-and-white ribbon ● white embroidery cotton and embroidery needle ● sewing thread ● synthetic stuffing

Method

Draw a 36 × 50cm (14¼ × 19¾in) rectangle on a sheet of paper. Draw an oval at the centre, 5–6cm (2–2⅜in) from the edges and then draw a cat silhouette in the centre. Cut out the oval pattern and use it to cut an oval from the white silk. Cut the cat from the black lace.

Cat Pin the lace cat to the centre of the silk. Secure it with large running stitches using white embroidery cotton. Pin the silk oval centrally to one of the black cotton rectangles. Pin the ribbon around the oval, covering the raw edges, and stitch down. Embroider the cat's eyes, nose and whiskers in white. Pleat the striped ribbon to make the collar, pin it in place and then stitch it securely. Sew the button to the centre of the collar.

Assembly Stitch the two black cotton rectangles together with right sides facing, 1.5cm (⅝in) from the edges, leaving a gap. Turn out through the gap and stuff. Close up the gap by hand.

Appliqué bear coat

Materials

Child's coat ● velvet and woollen fabric remnants ● machine sewing thread ● brown yarn and matching brown thread ● white chalk ● four wooden buttons for the eyes plus one for the heart

Method

Enlarge the patterns below to fit the coat. Cut out the large bear (head, body, arms, legs, ears and muzzle), the heart plus the stomach and one ear of the little bear from the different fabric remnants.

Big bear Position the big bear's pieces on the coat and attach using machine satin stitch around the edges.

Little bear Transfer the pattern for the little bear to the coat. Attach the stomach and ear as for the big bear then add the other contours by couching on the brown yarn with the matching thread.

Finishing Embroider the mouth and nose of each bear using straight stitch and satin stitch. Attach the wooden buttons for eyes. Neaten the edges of the heart with machine or hand stitching and use the final button to attach it to the coat.

Tip: Use fusible webbing, such as Bondaweb, to attach the body parts to the coat to hold them in place while you stitch.

Knitted ladybird toys

Dimensions

70 cm × 80 cm

Materials

1 ball each of pink, red and yellow cotton crochet/knitting yarn ● 4mm (UK 8, US 6) knitting needles (or size recommended by the yarn manufacturer for your chosen yarn) ● 1 bag of synthetic stuffing such as kapok ● 20mm (8in) felt circles for the large ladybird: 6 red and 6 pink ● 12mm (4¾in) felt circles for the small ladybird: 6 yellow and 6 red ● plain white knitted blanket

Method

Large ladybird Following the chart below, knit one ladybird in pink with a red head and red centre line, and one in red with a pink head and pink centre line. Small ladybird Following the chart below, knit one ladybird in red with a yellow head and yellow centre line and one in yellow with a red head and red centre line.

Antennae Using red, cast on 50 stitches for the large ladybird or 40 for the small one. Knit one row in red then one row in pink and cast off all the stitches in pink. Make two antennae for each ladybird.

Assembly Sew six felt circles on to each side of the ladybird in the same colour as the head and then sew the two knitted ladybird pieces together, leaving a gap at the top of the head end. Stuff the ladybirds. Roll the end of the antennas and fix with a few stitches then insert into the top of the ladybird and close up the gap.

Blanket Knit a selection of ladybirds following the chart and use white yarn to stitch them by hand to the white knitted blanket – the one shown is 70 × 80cm (27½ × 31½in). Embellish with hearts worked in chain stitch using leftover red and yellow yarn.

Tip: The white knitted blanket can be created quickly on a knitting machine, if you have one, and lengths can be joined as necessary.

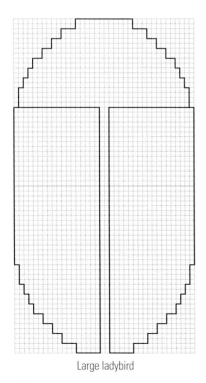

Large ladybird

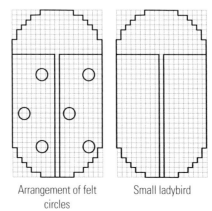

Arrangement of felt
circles

Small ladybird

Buttoned bear cushion

Dimensions

40 × 40cm (16 × 16in)

Materials

42cm (16½in) ecru braid, 5cm (2in) wide ● 20cm (8in) raw (unbleached) linen ● 50cm (½yd) striped canvas cloth ● 50cm (½yd) ecru linen cloth ● DMC stranded embroidery cotton in red 498, beige 640 and black ● four small mother-of-pearl buttons ● two small brown buttons for the eyes ● three 2cm (¾in) mother-of-pearl buttons for the cushion closure ● waste canvas ● sewing thread ● 40cm (16in) square cushion pad

Method

For the back of the cushion cover, cut one 46 × 42cm (18 × 16½in) rectangle from the ecru cloth. For the front, cut one 42cm (16½in) square from the striped cloth. Stitch the braid to the left edge of the square. Embroider three buttonholes, evenly spaced, in the braid.

Bear Enlarge the pattern for the bear to size (see page 2) and transfer the contours of the arms, legs, body and head to the linen cloth. Using the transparency of the fabric, transfer the surfaces to be embroidered to the waste canvas. Tack the waste canvas to the bear, positioning it carefully, and embroider using cross stitch with three strands of embroidery cotton. Pull away the waste canvas. Cut out each part of the bear, adding 1cm (⅜in) all round for seam allowances. Notch the seam allowances for ease and fold on to the wrong side, then attach to the striped top of the cushion with small stitches, beginning with the body. Attach the buttons to the bear, including the two for the eyes.

Assembly Place the two cushion pieces together with right sides facing and stitch together on three sides, leaving the edge with the braid open. Fold the excess fabric to the inside and stitch down. Attach the three large buttons to correspond with the buttonholes. Insert the suitable cushion pad and fasten the buttons.

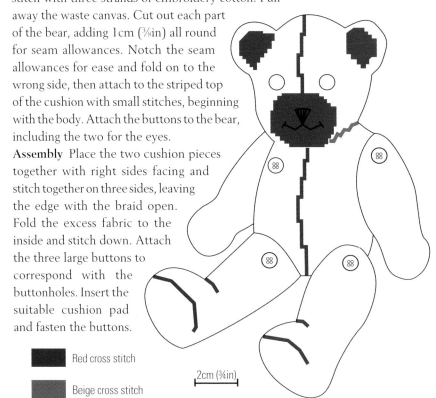

■ Red cross stitch

■ Beige cross stitch

2cm (¾in)

Dyed cat cushion

Dimensions

40 × 40cm (16 × 16in)

Materials

Two 44cm (17½in) squares of green boiled wool fabric ● unbleached linen fabric ● Dylon, multipurpose dye: coffee, Havana brown, old gold and olive green ● green sewing thread ● DMC stranded embroidery cotton in dark beaver grey 646 and very dark beaver grey 645 ● pins ● synthetic stuffing ● dressmakers' carbon paper ● tracing paper

Method

Dyeing Enlarge the pattern on pages 148–149 to size (see page 2) and trace off. Place the tracing paper on the linen to calculate the quantity of fabric to be dyed in each colour. Prepare a dark chocolate dye by mixing a little coffee dye and a lot of brown dye; for the light chocolate dye, mix a lot of coffee and little brown; for the brown dye, mix old gold and olive green with a little coffee dye. Dye the fabrics following the manufacturer's instructions. Leave to dry and then iron. Unravel each embroidery cotton to obtain a long thread. Soak one end in the coffee dye and the other in the brown dye, leaving the middle free to obtain a shaded thread.

Cat Place the tracing paper on the dyed fabric pieces and slide the carbon paper beneath. Draw over the contours to transfer the shapes and then cut them out. Pin the parts to each other, beginning with those at the back. Place the pieces on one of the green squares and attach them by embroidering in stem stitch using six strands of the embroidery cotton, 645 for the body and 646 for the head. Add the paw print in the bottom-left corner, using satin stitch to attach the pieces.

Assembly Place the two squares right sides together and stitch all round, taking a 2cm (¾in) seam allowance and leaving a gap in the middle of one side. Turn out and stuff. Close up the gap by hand.

Tip: If the idea of dyeing fabric puts you off, do not worry. You can still make the cushion using an assortment of brown fabric remnants.

Dyed cat cushion
(continued)

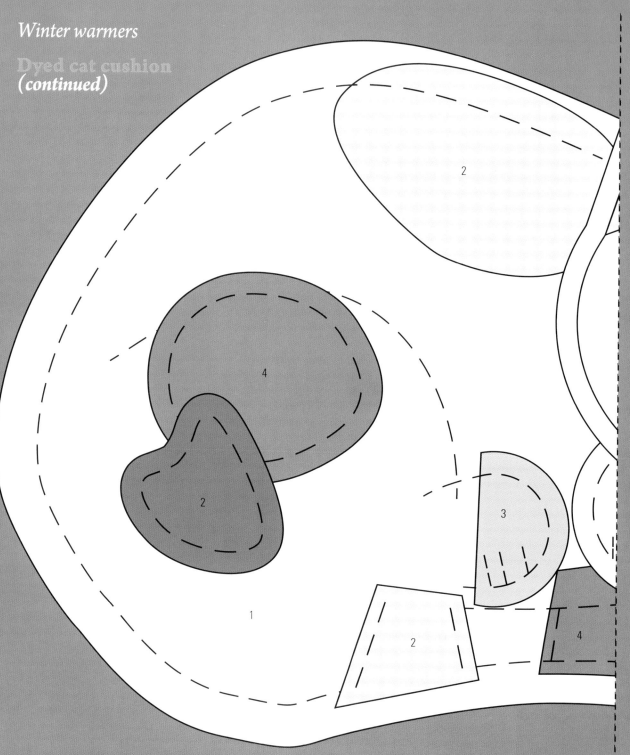

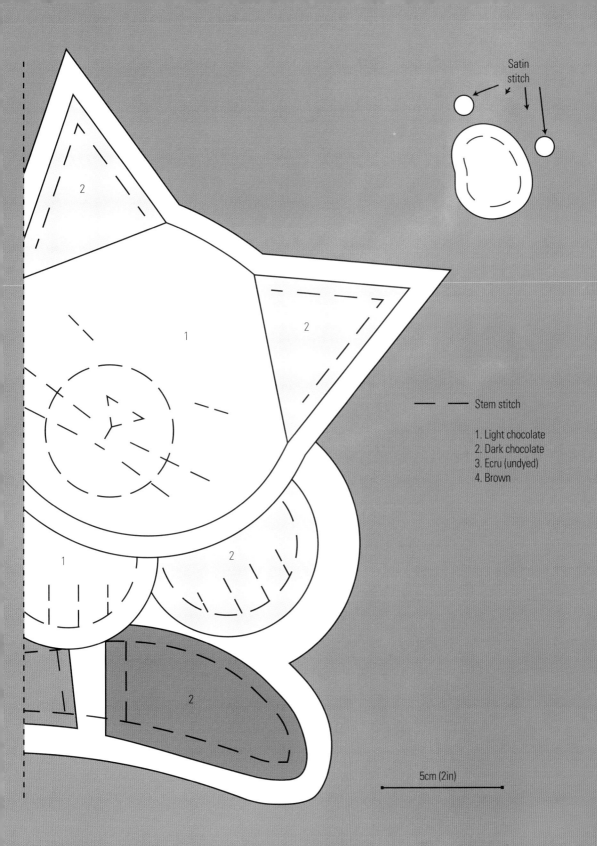

Satin stitch

– – – Stem stitch

1. Light chocolate
2. Dark chocolate
3. Ecru (undyed)
4. Brown

5cm (2in)

Skater-bear cushion

Dimensions

50 × 41cm (19¾ × 16in)

Materials

20cm (8in) each of off-white and sky-blue felt • 50cm (½yd) each of two checked woollen fabrics or one checked (for the front) and one plain (for the back) • crimping shears and straight scissors • DMC stranded embroidery cotton in light blue 813 • DMC Broder Machine (Brillante d'Alsace) thread in ecru • 20cm (8in) waste canvas • ballpoint pen • six buttons • scrap cardboard

Method

Using crimping shears, cut one 50 × 41cm (19¾ × 16in) rectangle of woollen fabric for the front and for the back cut one 16 × 41cm (6½ × 16in) rectangle and one 40 × 41cm (15¾ × 16in) rectangle. Make 1cm (⅜in) hems on one 41cm (16in) edge of each back piece.

Snow scene Trace the shapes of the bear, pine trees and circles on to cardboard to use as templates. Draw around the templates using a ballpoint pen on the wrong side of the felt and the top piece. Cut out the pine trees, the bear and his scarf with straight scissors and the circles with the crimping shears. Tack in place then fix with small cross stitches in ecru or blue thread. Trace the lines of the ice on a strip of waste canvas. Tack the canvas 12cm (4¾in) from the bottom of the front piece and then embroider with cross stitch using three strands of blue thread. Pull away the canvas. Secure the circles with the buttons, tying the blue thread through the buttonholes and leaving the thread ends hanging free for decoration. Embroider a few cross stitches on the top circles.

Assembly Lay out the top piece, right side down and lay the back pieces right side up on top with the raw edges matching and the hemmed edges overlapping in the centre. Pin the layers together then stitch all round, 2cm (¾in) from the edges, selecting a decorative machine stitch.

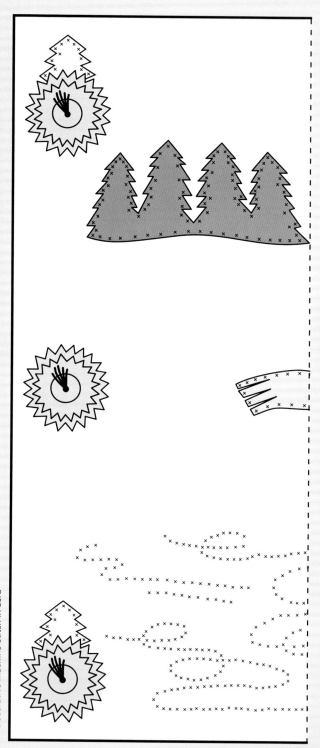

Decorative machine stitch in ecru

5cm (2in)

Bear appliqué scarf

Materials

1 green scarf ● fabric remnants including beige fabric for the body ● transfer pencil ● sheet of tracing paper ● sewing thread ● DMC pearl cotton No. 3 in bright red 666 ● DMC stranded embroidery cotton in old gold 729, dark beaver grey 646, Delft blue 809 and black 310

Method

Enlarge the pattern below to size (see page 2), trace the bear body shapes and transfer them to the beige fabric. Cut out, adding 3mm (⅛in) all round. Sew on to the scarf, folding the 3mm (⅛in) seam allowance towards the wrong side with the point of the needle as you go. Cut out the clothing pieces and attach them in the same way over the body, working from the lowest fabrics upwards. Embroider the facial features and details of the clothes using stem stitch, French knots and topstitch following the patterns.

1	= 666 red
2	= 729 old gold
3	= 646 dark grey
4	= 809 blue
5	= 310 balck
ᴏᴏ	= Stem stitch
o	= French not
—	= Backstitch

3cm (1¼in)

Stargazing bears

Dimensions

84 × 122cm (33 × 48in)

Materials

90×130cm (35½×51in) rectangle of wadding (batting) ● 90×130cm (35½×51in) rectangle of cotton fabric for the backing ● various cotton fabrics for the front, appliqué work and borders ● quilting needle ● appliqué needle ● scissors ● pins

Method

Enlarge the pattern on page 158 to size. Cut out an 86 × 124cm (34 × 49in) rectangle of wadding. From assorted cotton fabrics cut the strips of the edges and rectangles of the base, adding 1cm (⅜in) seam allowances. The pieces are appliquéd to the wadding so pin the parts in place on the wadding, beginning with those of the base and folding the seam allowances to the wrong side for the edges which remain on the top, where the parts overlap. Sew with running stitch or backstitch and contrasting coloured thread.

Bears Cut out the different parts of the bears, adding 1cm (⅜in) seam allowances. Fold the seam allowances to the wrong side then attach in place using irregular straight stitches, always beginning with the background pieces. Embroider the eyes, nose and mouth of each bear, and any other detailing with satin stitch and the background stars with backstitch.

Stars and moon Attach the appliqué stars and moon in the same way as for the bears, using the pattern as your guide.

Assembly Lay out the finished piece, right side up and pin the backing fabric right side down on top. Stitch all round, 2cm (⅜in) from the edges, leaving a gap to turn through. Trim the seam allowances at the corners. Turn out and close the gap with small hand stitching.

Tip: You may find it easier to cut the pieces for the bears, stars and moon without seam allowances, fuse them to the quilt top using fusible webbing, such as Bondaweb, and then machine stitch the pieces in place with narrow zigzag over the edges.

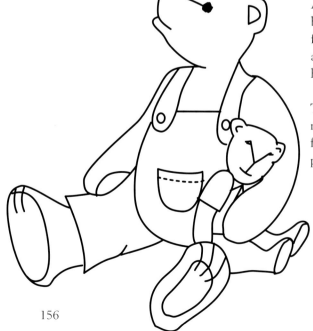

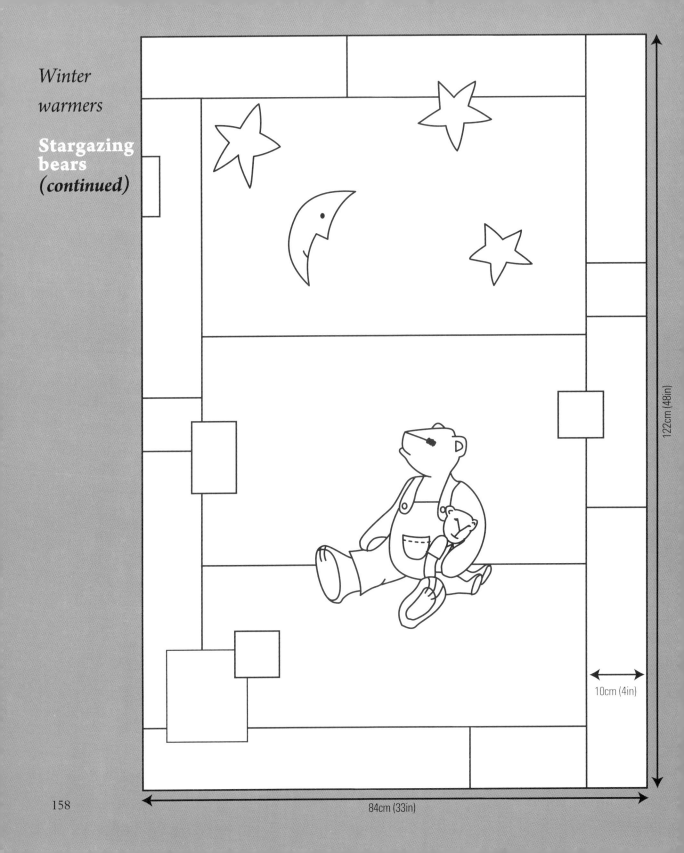

84cm (33in)

122cm (48in)

10cm (4in)

Credits

First published in Great Britain 2012 by Search Press Limited,
Wellwood, North Farm Road, Tunbridge Wells, Kent TN2 3DR

Original title: *Animaux en tissu, 50 modèles à coudre*

© 2011 by Éditions Marie Claire – Société d'Information et de Créations (SIC)

English translation by Karen Murphy at Cicero Translations

English edition typeset by GreenGate Publishing Services

ISBN: 978-1-84448-770-7

Graphic design and layout: Either studio
Instructions: Renée Méry
Patterns: Nadine Sevin